M000044889

Other Books by the Authors

BUT IF NOT, VOLUME I

BUT IF NOT, VOLUME III
(AVAILABLE MARCH 2009)

JESUS WEPT

LOSS AND GRIEF RECOVERY

But If Not

But If Not

ENDURING LOSS, ILLNESS, AND DEATH

Volume Two

Joyce and Dennis Ashton

CFI

Springville, Utah

© 2008 Joyce and Dennis Ashton
All rights reserved.

No part of this book may be reproduced in any form whatsoever, whether by graphic, visual, electronic, film, microfilm, tape recording, or any other means, without prior written permission of the publisher, except in the case of brief passages embodied in critical reviews and articles.

This is not an official publication of The Church of Jesus Christ of Latter-day Saints. The opinions and views expressed herein belong solely to the author and do not necessarily represent the opinions or views of Cedar Fort, Inc. Permission for the use of sources, graphics, and photos is also solely the responsibility of the author.

ISBN 13: 978-1-59955-240-8

Published by CFI, an imprint of Cedar Fort, Inc., 2373 W. 700 S., Springville, UT 84663
Distributed by Cedar Fort, Inc., www.cedarfort.com

LIBRARY OF CONGRESS CATALOGING-IN-PUBLICATION DATA

Ashton, Joyce.
 But if not : enduring loss, illness, and death, Vol. 2 / Joyce and
Dennis Ashton.
  p. cm.
 ISBN 978-1-59955-240-8
 1. Suffering--Religious aspects--Church of Jesus Christ of Latter-day
Saints. 2. Suffering--Religious aspects--Mormon Church. I. Ashton, Dennis,
1950- II. Title.

 BX8643.S93A83 2008
 248.8'6--dc22

                                                            2008010772

Cover design by Angela Olsen
Cover design © 2008 by Lyle Mortimer

Printed in the United States of America

10 9 8 7 6 5 4 3 2 1

Printed on acid-free paper

TO

Darren D. Ashton

WHO INSPIRED THE BUT IF NOT
TITLE THROUGH HIS SUFFERING,
FAITH, AND ENDURING

CONTENTS

Preface

THIS IS VOLUME II OF OUR *BUT IF NOT* SERIES. In this volume we will address coping with disabilities; chronic, terminal, and mental illnesses; and the death of a loved one. The first volume discusses the grief symptoms that you may experience as you encounter any type of loss or life challenge. Volume I also offers healing interventions to help you cope with your loss.

Dennis and I learned about loss and grief early in our marriage when we experienced infertility, followed by the death of our first full-term, seven-pound baby daughter. We started writing about grief years later after the death of our disabled fourteen-year-old son, Cameron. It was our oldest son Darren's enduring and faith during his two-year illness that inspired the title *But If Not*.

Additional losses and life's challenges have inevitably continued to roll into our family's lives, such as miscarriage, disability, deaths, addictions, illness, and other life challenges. Each of our lives is full of joy, loss, sadness, and hope, all woven together. Our personal challenge is to remain faithful, find meaning, and choose to carry on in the face of our own unique trials and adversities. The *But If Not* series is offered as a guide and support for you and those you love as you cope with personal challenges and help them cope with theirs.

We wish you ultimate happiness and healing on life's journey. It is our hope and prayer that the lessons, techniques, and spiritual insights we have learned as fellow travelers will, in some beneficial way, ease your suffering.

—Joyce and Dennis Ashton

CHAPTER ONE

Disabilities, Physical and Mental Illness

THE TITLE *BUT IF NOT* IS SPUN FROM THE ILLNESS of our oldest adult son, Darren. A few years ago he had a colon mass removed, which resulted in severe complications and several major surgeries. Through his suffering, Dennis and I came to appreciate more deeply a favorite scripture that we would quote to each other when one of us got discouraged.

The scripture tells a powerful story about three righteous and brave men. Shadrach, Meshach, and Abed-nego were to be thrown into a "burning fiery furnace" for worshipping God. They displayed their commitment and faith by replying, "Our God whom we serve is able to deliver us. . . . *But if not*, be it known . . . that we will not serve thy gods, nor worship the golden image" (Daniel 3:17–18; emphasis added).

In response to the story of Shadrach, Meshach, and Abed-nego, Elder Dennis E. Simmons reminds us:

> We must have the same faith as Shadrach, Meshach, and Abed-nego. Our God will deliver us from ridicule and persecution, but if not . . . from sickness and disease, from loneliness, depression, or fear, but if not . . . Our God will deliver us from threats, accusations, insecurity, death or impairment . . . He will make sure that we are loved and recognized, receive a perfect companion and righteous and obedient children, but if not, we will have faith in the Lord Jesus Christ, knowing that IF we do all we can do, we will, in His time and in his way, be delivered and receive all that He has.[1]

Whether it is for a physical ailment or a mental illness, the diagnosis of a disability for you or a loved one can result in a major loss and the need to make significant adjustments in your life. Although you may feel you clearly understand that our journey on earth includes confronting illness and suffering, it may still come as a shock when you personally have to assimilate and deal with a serious diagnosis and a life-altering tragedy.

Dennis and I still remember the vivid details associated with receiving the varied diagnoses that accompanied our own children's disabilities and illnesses. We will never forget the shock when our doctor told us that our first seven-pound, full-term baby girl had died. It was our first conceived child after a season of infertility. We could hardly believe what had happened as we looked at her beautiful but lifeless body. A cause for her death was never determined.

A few years later the doctor confirmed that our third child, Cameron, had cerebral palsy. We weren't sure what it would mean to parent such a child. After fourteen years of learning how to feed and care for him, we were heartbroken at his sudden and unexpected death.

We were shaken again when I experienced a TIA, or mini-stroke, at age forty-seven. I woke up in the middle of the night and couldn't move the left side of my body. Although I recovered, I've faced several fearful years as experts attempted to determine a cause, including the discovery of what appears to be MS lesions on my brain.

It was surreal five years later when our oldest, now adult son, Darren, became ill and required several major surgeries. We have other close family members whose struggles with mental illnesses have resulted in drug and alcohol addictions. The negative consequences and their associated behaviors have taken a toll financially, emotionally, and spiritually for our family members. Dennis's mother took her own life at age fifty after overdosing on prescription drugs and alcohol.

Dennis and I have found comfort in the stories and insight given to us by others who have coped with difficult diagnoses. Job comes to mind as well as Paul with his "thorn in the side." We have also been impressed with President Spencer W. Kimball's thoughts on adversity. Much of what he learned was a by-product of his own profound suffering and personal life experiences. He, like Job, suffered from boils. He also experienced skin cancer, Bell's palsy, smallpox, and heart pain for years, which eventually required open-heart surgery. He endured three brain surgeries. He suffered skin and throat cancer, which necessitated vocal cord surgery and ultimately led to his difficulty speaking.[2]

Physical and mental illnesses and disabilities affect the family as a whole and each member individually. If you have ever watched someone you love suffer, you now realize that you not only grieve for the dying, but you also grieve for the living.

Physical or Chronic Illness

There are many illnesses and diseases that we might acquire in our lifetime. Living with chronic pain and symptoms is a challenge.

Some individuals who are suffering significant physical or emotional pain report that they would rather die than continue in their suffering. Those watching at the bedside as caregivers may feel similarly. Caregivers, especially parents, often wish they could take the place of their suffering loved one. One mother said, "I would have gladly suffered in place of my son. There is nothing worse than watching someone you love suffer and not be able to change their painful experience."

Our sister-in-law said, "When my mother told me about her

cancer I was twelve years old. I was so upset. I ran to my friend's house crying all the way! I just knew she [my mother] would immediately die. This experience, hearing of mother's diagnosis, was more difficult for me than her death seven years later."[3]

This quote reveals that sometimes anticipatory mourning and preparation can soften the impact when death eventually does arrive.

Adolescents are often embarrassed by a parent's or sibling's illness, disability, or appearance. A mother with cancer illustrates this embarrassment: "One day I had to make a quick run to my child's school. I just threw on a baseball hat to cover my bald head. When my child got home from school, he asked if I would please wear my wig when I came to the school."

One of our patients suffering from cancer told of her child's embarrassment: "I lost all my hair during chemotherapy. Sometimes I would take my wig off and swing it around being silly. One of my children would laugh, but the other would ask me to please not do it."

These reactions and comments may later cause the embarrassed individual to feel guilty, especially if the loved one dies from the illness. Discussing ambivalent feelings and helping families realize their mixed, and at times conflicting emotions, may help them eventually abandon their guilt.

Occasionally our children were embarrassed when our large family would all go out to eat. Cameron was in his wheelchair, and we would have to feed him because it would be too messy if he tried to feed himself in public. His brothers were self-conscious when they perceived others were critically judging them as well as Cameron.

For many, the emotional suffering can be as intense as physical suffering. Each new day can introduce a new set of emotions. These emotions are influenced by medical treatments, test results, and current health status. Individuals' reactions are also influenced and weighed against the quality and anticipated duration of life. A dear friend and relative told us years ago: "My cancer experience left me emotionally drained and severely depressed. There were times it was more than I could bear, and I wanted to die. If my cancer returns I will not go through all the treatments again. I will just take pain medication until I die. I am not afraid of physical pain; it's the emotional pain that I cannot do again."

I don't think Dennis or I totally understood her painful, emotional recovery until we watched Darren's recovery from what turned out to be several serious abdominal surgeries and months of complications and hospitalizations. There were many times we feared we would be burying our third child. It brought back our grief memories and vulnerability as we remembered our previous son Cameron's surgery and death. It was a long recovery. We found that long after the physical healing was done there was emotional and psychological grief to heal from as well. The long-term effects of emotional recovery were described well by Lance Armstrong.

This is what he said a year following his cancer remission: "I was physically recovered, but my soul was still healing. There is no support system in place to deal with the emotional ramifications of trying to return to the world after living in a bottle for your existence."[4]

A part of him didn't want to return to his old life. He wanted a permanent vacation. Darren felt similarly as he fought to come back. He had good days and bad days and wondered if he would ever be the same again. We knew in reality that most individuals wouldn't be the same after such suffering. Loss and life's challenges change us. We see through different eyes.

The constant ups and downs of remissions and relapses can be exhausting. Dennis and I would think Darren was out of the woods, and then he would get another infection with a fever and painful, intense cramps. We would all sink into fear and despair thinking he might have to go back to the hospital. What if he didn't make it this time? I told him I understood the phrase, "A mother is only as happy as her saddest child."

Illness can cause spiritual injury. We may ask, "Why me? Why hasn't God intervened and healed me? Where is my miracle? Why does He allow me to continue to suffer?" In the midst of Darren's suffering and surgeries, Dennis and I would return to the scriptural passage that helped us cope. We determined that we would continue to hope and pray for a healing, "But if not . . ." we will still remain faithful (Daniel 3:17–18).

Other times during our struggles we may see that someone's spirituality increases. A friend of ours told us, "Since my adversity, I am just loving going to church and lapping up every spiritual moment and lesson I can."

When we first began working with individuals who were suffering from serious illnesses, we assumed we would always see chronic sorrow and depression. However, as with life in general, some patients are able to cope better and discover personal meaning at varying stages in their tragedies and losses. Reactions are in fact very individualized, especially when observed as single moments in time. Conclusions and feedback concerning how well someone is coping in the early stage of mourning often discourages people from honestly sharing their struggles later when their grief returns.

A while back I was visiting a family of seven whose young father was dying after a long, chronic illness. His beautiful wife sat crying at his bedside. The care center and hospice staff worried about her grief. She had a son serving a mission and four younger children still at home. However, her tears were tears of gratitude for the powerful comfort and the Spirit she was feeling. She told me, "I am not a strong person; I am being carried." She had received spiritual peace and was ready to let her husband transcend to his next life. At that moment she was embraced with the overwhelming love of the Savior. She did go through a more typical grief process later. For that time, however, she acknowledged that she was in the arms of her Lord. It's important to validate the spiritual comfort and support an individual may receive, while leaving an invitation to share painful moments that may resurface in the future.

I hadn't totally understood the enormous comfort a grieving individual can receive until I experienced it personally. In the midst of Darren's serious complications from surgeries, I was still able to find peace, comfort, and answers to prayers. It was an amazing experience for me. I understood more fully how the Lord, without removing our trials, can comfort and carry us through them. By discovering these "tender mercies" (1 Nephi 1:20), we will more likely find meaning and peace in our suffering.

Disabilities

Dennis and I came to understand and glimpse into the world of the disabled through Cameron. When he was ten months old, he could not sit up without assistance. The doctor sent a nurse to our home to test the extent of his developmental delays. After she left (although she never gave us a diagnosis) the term *cerebral palsy* came to my mind. I looked it up in my college nursing book and recognized that his delays and birth injuries fit the diagnosis. Receiving the diagnosis of a disability can begin an intense grieving process, and for me, it did. I remember closing the drapes, taking the phone off the hook, and crying uncontrollably. How could we raise a disabled child? What did this mean for our lives?

Later the doctor confirmed the diagnosis. We made many

adjustments and over the years learned to care for him. Our lives suddenly included wheelchairs, daily dressing, feeding, toileting, bathing, and countless doctor visits.

The mother of a blind child said, "My child could see normally for many years and had many friends in and out of the Church. After she lost her vision she also lost her friends. It was very difficult for both of us."

The mother of a disabled baby writes:

> When you get pregnant, it's like planning a fabulous trip to a place you've dreamed of all your life, maybe . . . to Italy. You buy a bunch of guide books and make wonderful plans. It's all very exciting. After months of eager anticipation, the day finally arrives. You pack your bags and off you go. Several hours later, the plane lands. The stewardess says, "Welcome to Holland." "What!? I signed up for Italy. . . . I've wanted to go there all my life!" "Well there's been a change in the flight plan, and here you must stay!" It's not a horrible place, just different than you expected. You must learn a different language. And everyone you know is talking about their trip to Italy, and how wonderful it is there. "Yes," you say, I was supposed to go there too. The pain of this change will never go away, the loss of your dream. I will try and see the beautiful things in Holland. They do have tulips and windmills![5]

There are often secondary losses along the way. A young father writes, "I've spent most of my life working hard to get good grades and a good career. I married and started my family before I finished law school. I finally got a job offer with the company of my dreams; however, I couldn't accept it due to the serious illness and disabilities of my child."

Accidents can cause disabilities, adding guilt to our intense grief. One person said, "In a flash I went from a healthy, active young adult to a paraplegic. The panic of not being able to feel and move eventually turned to sorrow. I had to alter all of my goals and plans. It took every ounce of physical, emotional, and spiritual strength to go on."

When Cameron was diagnosed, Dennis and I wondered how we, or anyone, would accept this less than "normal" child. Would he accept himself? Like most parents, we wanted to ensure that he had the opportunity to be the best he could be. We wanted to give Cameron every opportunity available. The professionals could not tell for sure if he would ever walk, so we worked long and hard assuming he would. It took many years for us to realize he would not. We learned that his cognitive and physical growth would be a slow process, and that small accomplishments in those areas would measure his and our successes. The doctors didn't feel that he would be able to talk, so we taught him how to use a communication board. He learned to use it very fast, and then surprised us by developing language skills and eventually speaking.

Here is what I wrote regarding his growth:

> Cameron's first partial sentence was a small miracle to us. He was three years old and this was the first day that he would go to a special preschool without mom, all alone on a bus. As

I was dressing him I could see the anxiety in his eyes. His big brown eyes always melted my heart. He looked up at me and asked, "Mamma go?" Tears came to my eyes and I cheered, "You spoke, you spoke!" With great emotion I explained he would be going to school alone, but I would be home when he returned. We were going to have some great communication together and make the most of his limitations! He had communicated and I had understood! This was such a great thrill![6]

It wasn't long before patient friends and relatives could understand Cameron's slurred speech, which replaced his need to use the communication board. We were all thrilled and grateful when others at home, church, and school could understand him over time.

Other parents will have disabled children who will never speak with words. These parents will have to look for other qualities within their children's personalities and spirits that can bring them joy. If they are able to focus on their child's inner qualities, or self-worth, and the importance of their child's existence as a child of God, they will find meaning and purpose.

Caregiving can be very difficult and demanding for families. There is usually more to do than feels humanly possible. Often we can't find or accept all the help we need or desire. A mother writes that after finding little support during her son's illness that she became immersed in the work of caring for him. Over time she was unable to attend to anything else. "I am the main caregiver.

My husband doesn't really do much of the necessary care. He has thrown himself into his work and earning the money to enable me to stay at home. This has caused some arguments, because if he would give some of the medications or treatments, I could have a break, or eat hot food!"[7]

Although most of the time my family remained positive, there were some challenges we faced in caring for our disabled son. The following is an entry from my journal when he started school:

> I have been helping Cameron in his classroom. I worry when I see him with other normal children. He doesn't fit in very well. It's sad and emotional for me to watch. It's hard at home too; lifting, feeding and bathing him. Sometimes I get down and discouraged. One day Cameron asked me, "Why am I handicapped anyway? I said, "It's our challenge." He said, "I wanta be normal. I wanta walk, I wanta walk!" I did the best I could to comfort him. I sometimes feel sad for him and for me.

Over the years Dennis and I had learned to accept Cameron's disability and love him immensely. Although it was hard work, we found joy and purpose in caring for him. We spent nearly every day for fourteen years feeding, bathing, and dressing him. And we spent every day addressing his medical and emotional needs. He attended special schools. He was happy and loved living. We spent countless hours trying to find the right wheelchairs, computer, electric bed, prone standing table, eating utensils, and school programs for him.

JOYCE AND DENNIS ASHTON

At age fourteen, six months before his death, Cameron
expressed the following ideas and feelings to a class of college students majoring in special education. It took an hour to videotape
this fourteen-minute testimony because of his labored speech and
limited grammar:

> Hi! My name is Cameron Ashton, and I live at Dallas,
> Texas, and this is my house and this is my pool. I can swim
> with a little help from this [holds up arm floats]. It really neat.
> It a hot day here. I have a trampoline. It over there [points], and
> I can jump on it, and I mean I can lay on it and have somebody
> jump with me [his honesty]. And I have a bike I can use, and it's
> in the garage. [We get it out for him.] This is my bike that I ride.
> I ride it to the duck pond. It a little ways from here and my dad
> helps me get on and my mom too, and it really fun to ride. It like
> walking for me. Plus my family is really nice too. My dad helps
> me get dressed in the morning and helps me go bathroom and
> all that. And I have aide who work good [at] school, helps me at
> school [his appreciation], and my school is across the street, and
> my mom helps me a lot. She helps me with my homework.
>   It not easy being handicapped. It look easy, but not really.
> It like hard, I guess [realistic]. [But] I get to drive early [finds
> the positive]! I'll drive it [moves the wheelchair around]. I hope
> I can go on a mission and be married in the temple. Sometimes
> hard for me to be handicapped, like for example, I can't play
> basketball and football like you guys can do. I can't *do* a lot,
> but I play with my computer [he finds the positive again], and
> I hope to learn more about the computer and so I can teach my
> mom and my dad to use it and stuff. [We learned how to use
> it!] I hope you can understand me okay and learn what it like to

14

be handicapped. . . . I really like Texas, I moved here just a year or two ago, and I like it so far. It big and nice and I really like it. It [Texas] good. Here, oh boy. Here my suggestions about college helpers of handicapped people. Be nice to handicapped. They know a lot just like you, and don't tease handicapped people because it hurt their feelings. I LDS boy and that mean I go to church every Sunday, like today, I just came back from church. . . . I guess I don't have to say anymore, and this is Cameron signing off. (See his concluding testimony on page 79.)[8]

Words cannot describe the profound grief and loss we experienced following his death.

Mental Illnesses

Just as physical illness affects and limits our physical bodies, mental illness can affect and limit our brain's capacity to think clearly and control our emotions. Mental illness can compromise our thoughts, feelings, behaviors, and how we interact with others.

> The truth is that many faithful Latter-day Saints, who live the commandments and honor their covenants, experience personal struggles with mental illness, or are required to deal, perhaps over long periods of time, with the intense pain and suffering of morally righteous mentally ill family members. I assure you that Church leaders are in no way exempt from the burden of mental illness, whether as victim, caregiver, or friend.[9]

Experts do not totally understand why some people's brains

malfunction. However, faulty brain function is as real as cancer, physical disabilities, or diseases of any vital body organ. Mental illness is usually not caused by sin, cannot be willed away, and often requires professional treatment. Some of the more commonly recognized mental illnesses include depression, anxiety disorders, obsessive-compulsive disorder, bipolar disorder, schizophrenia, attention deficit disorder, and eating disorders. We will define these mental conditions later in the chapter.

Mental illness is usually not as visible as physical illnesses; however, the suffering and impact is just as profound for the patient and the patient's family.

"Most patients would rather have a physical than a mental disorder. . . . Among the more important reasons . . . is the fact that psychological diagnosis often carries a stigma, as many still believe that a psychological problem implies that a person is weak and has not tried hard enough to overcome the problem."[10]

Unfortunately, because of a lack of knowledge and understanding, few families receive cards, flowers, or casseroles when a mental crisis hits or sends a family member to the hospital. It is important for friends, family, and ward members to increase their knowledge and acceptance relative to the complete causes and impact of mental illnesses. The mentally ill and their families desperately need our nonjudgmental love, support, and acceptance.

Many mental illnesses go untreated because individuals are

ashamed, in denial, or feel their symptoms can be willed away with their positive attitude.

One woman tells of her struggle being married to a man with a severe mental illness: "I married a returned missionary who I thought had left his past and struggles with adolescence. Unfortunately his mental illness continues to resurface in our marriage. The loss of what I thought marriage and family life would be has left me with a grief I can't describe. I'm not sure I have what it takes to stay married to a spouse with so many problems."

Another person says, "I had no time to study for my bar exam due to the serious mental illness of my spouse. I had to pursue a different career."

The following eleven mental health conditions are frequently diagnosed and treated in LDS Family Services. Personal quotes illustrate some of the difficulties faced by individuals suffering and those who love them. Understanding the diagnosis and symptoms is the first step to healing.

Obsessive-Compulsive Disorder: Unwanted intrusive and recurrent impulses, images, or thoughts that one cannot control (obsessions). Repetitive behaviors or mental acts that the person feels driven to perform in response to an obsession (compulsions).[11]

"Before I can leave the house I have several rituals that I must do in a certain order. I try logically to stop but cannot."

"I am so obsessive about certain unimportant details of my life that it keeps me from doing the truly important things and finding contentment or joy."

Major Depressive Disorder: Depressed mood lasting most the day nearly every day. Many people suffering from depression experience changes in sleep, libido, appetite, or weight, as well as a loss of pleasure, interest, or motivation in activities they once enjoyed. They can also experience a loss of energy, hope, and worth. An inability to concentrate, focus, or function as usual is also common. People suffering from depression may be more tearful, irritable, or indecisive. Feelings of anxiety or guilt, or thoughts of suicide, are common.[12]

"My depression limits my ability to give to my family. I hide in my room, reading or sleeping, isolating myself from everyone and everything."

Generalized Anxiety Disorder: Exaggerated worry and restlessness generally lasting for six months or longer. One may experience headaches, dizziness, blackouts, and a difficulty breathing or swallowing. Some may feel nervous, tense, sweaty, or even experience heart palpitations. Some may suffer from panic attacks, which are sudden feelings of terror that often occur unexpectedly.[13]

"I feel anxious about everything: work, school, and friends. I worry I will have a full-blown panic attack one of these days."

Personality Disorders: Enduring patterns of inner experiences and behavior that deviate markedly from cultural expectations. These patterns appear in the following areas: cognitions, affectivity, interpersonal functioning and impulse control. There is a general criteria for personality disorders and those not specific; others are called borderline, paranoid, schizoid, antisocial, histrionic, narcissistic, avoidant, and dependent personality disorders.[14]

Adjustment Disorders: The development of emotional or behavioral symptoms in response to an identifiable stressor(s).[15]

"When I went back to work at the children's ward at the hospital after the death of my child, I started feeling uncomfortable. Sometimes I felt anxiety and panic, fearing I would be responsible for a child's death. I worried my fear could turn into PTSD [posttraumatic stress disorder] so I changed units."

Attention Deficit/Hyperactivity Disorder (ADHD): Common symptoms may include restlessness, fidgetiness, the inability to sit still, the ability to become distracted easily, impulsivity, forgetfulness, and impatience. Those with ADHD often struggle with saying and doing things before thinking. They also have trouble staying focused on tasks or thoughts. Many experience extreme mood shifts from normal to depressed to excited feelings in a short period of time. Some associated features include marital instability, a lack of academic and vocational success, stress intolerance, and alcohol and drug abuse.

"My daughter's ADHD has led her to very negative behaviors. Her teachers call and complain about her conduct. She has trouble keeping friends, making appropriate decisions, and keeping her grades up."

Bipolar Disorder: Alternating periods of depression and manic euphoria. In most cases euphoria is an elevated or irritable mood.[16]

"My daughter will go days with little sleep. Excited about life and goals she wants to accomplish. She seems overly excited and somewhat unrealistic about what she is involved with. Then she crashes and sleeps for days or is unmotivated and depressed."

Delusional Disorder: At least a one-month duration of real life, nonbizarre situations that are delusional. Examples might include the fear of being poisoned, infected, or deceived by a spouse or loved one.[17]

"It took months of therapy to convince my husband that his bizarre thoughts were unfounded. He believed our temple marriage of forty years was being threatened by me being unfaithful to him."

Conduct Disorders: There are different types of conduct disorders. However, it is usually a persistent pattern of behavior where the rights of others or rules are violated.[18]

"My son's conduct disorder began as a young child. He was cruel to animals and experimented with fire. He has spent multiple times in jail."

Eating Disorders: Eating disorders are a complex way to manage emotions. There are three types described here. (1) Anorexia

Nervosa: Forced extreme weight loss (25 percent or more of body fat) causing life-threatening symptoms due to severe malnutrition and excessive exercise. Even with extreme thinness, patients believe they are fat. (2) Bulimia Nervosa: Extreme overeating, bingeing, and then purging, which is forced vomiting. Victims may also over-use laxatives and other weight loss products. (3) Binge Eating Disorder: Uncontrolled, impulsive continual eating beyond the point of feeling full. Food addictions (without purging) causing gains up to 50 percent over normal weight.[19] Binge eating disorder produces physical changes in the brain similar to those of drug abuse.

"I used to be thin; I started putting on extra weight last year. I love to eat, but I started to cut back what calories I could. Soon I would overeat and binge, then purge to control my weight. I ruined my throat, hair, and emotional peace."

Schizophrenia: Hallucinations (hearing or seeing things that don't actually exist), delusions, paranoia, and disordered speech and thoughts.

"I have been called by God to travel the world, preaching his word."

Professional resources include your local LDS Family Service agency, faithful Latter-day Saints in public and private practice, the NAMI (National Alliance on Mental Illness) organization, your county mental health agency, and The National Institute of Mental Health (NIMH) 866-615-6464.

Treating these illnesses can be effective, yet complicated. There are studies that compare the effectiveness of psychotherapy such as cognitive, behavior, and interpersonal therapies with and without medication for each illness. It would be impossible to review all the research in this chapter. However, it would be important to seek education and counseling for your specific illness. Most research confirms that medications and psychotherapy are equally effective in treating mental illnesses. However, if both are initiated and used in concert, therapy outcome improves substantially.

"Some persons who are ill, who have received a priesthood blessing and have prayed fervently that their burdens might be lightened, may feel that they suffer from a lamentable lack of faith if they seek professional help for their affliction. They may even stop taking prescribed medication, thinking erroneously that their faith will replace the need for it. Such thinking is quite simply wrong. Receiving and acting upon professional advice and the concomitant exercise of faith are not in conflict. In fact, exercising faith may require following the advice of experienced health professionals."[20]

For spiritual and emotional self-help tools and interventions, see *But If Not, Volume I*.

Notes

1. Dennis E. Simmons, "But If Not . . .," *Ensign*, May 2004, 73.
2. James E. Faust, "The Blessings of Adversity," *Ensign*, February 1998, 2–7.

3. Joyce and Dennis Ashton, *Jesus Wept* (Springville, Utah: Cedar Fort, Inc., 2001), 31.
4. Lance Armstrong with Salley Jenkins, *It's Not About the Bike: My Journey Back to Life*, audio book (New York: Penguin Putman Inc., 2000).
5. E. Kingsley, "Welcome to Holland" broadcast by Television Works Western Publication Co., 508-750-8400.
6. Joyce and Dennis Ashton, *Loss and Grief Recovery* (Amityville, New York: Baywood Publishing, 1996), 51.
7. Ibid., 26.
8. Ibid., 64.
9. Alexander B. Morrison, "Myths about Mental Illness," *Ensign*, October 2005, 31–35.
10. Elliot S. Valenstein, *Blaming the Brain* (New York: The Free Press, 1998), 219.
11. DSM-IV-TR American Psychiatric Association, Washington DC, 2000, 217–18.
12. Ibid., 168–69.
13. Ibid., 222–23.
14. Ibid., 287.
15. Ibid., 285.
16. Ibid., 179–91.
17. Ibid., 159–60.
18. Ibid., 68–69.
19. Ibid., 263–66.
20. Elder Alexander B. Morrison, "The Spiritual Component of Healing," *Ensign*, June 2008, 47.

CHAPTER TWO

Terminal Illness

WE WORKED ON THIS CHAPTER TWO WEEKS after the death of our dear mother. She came to live with us three months ago on hospice care. She received a terminal diagnosis of inflammatory breast cancer six months before her death. Caring for her was an honor and a privilege. We had a few hard days, but not many. She was the perfect patient, always grateful for everything that was done for her. We hope to endure to the end as well as she has.

A terminal illness is a diagnosis of a disease that will take the life of an individual. Usually it refers to a time period of weeks or months rather than years. One of the most common diseases we see in hospice is cancer. Most of us will know someone who will suffer with cancer. Cancer is not always terminal. Over eight million people are living today with a history of cancer. An additional 1.2 million will be diagnosed this year.[1]

Terminal illness is uniquely different from chronic illness because those affected must now shift from hope for a cure to hope for comfort, peace, and a good death. Focus changes from earth life to eternal life and includes letting go of earthly things. Embracing the idea of death can be a challenge for the dying as well as for their families. Dying is a unique and individual process. Transcending from earth life to a hereafter will involve physical, mental, social, spiritual, and emotional work. We may have to sacrifice what we are for what we will become. This process can be complicated as patients and families struggle to do important end-of-life tasks that may include offering forgiveness, asking for forgiveness, expressing love, saying thank you, and ultimately saying good-bye.

It may take a while for the diagnosis of death to sink in. Some patients actually die with the belief that they aren't dying and thus miss the opportunity to complete important end-of-life tasks. Others wonder, "Do I really have to die?" or "Has my life made a difference?" Many question, "Why, God? Why me? Why suffering?" Half of those facing immediate death worry about not being forgiven by God and not reconciling with others.[2] Others express fears about approaching the unknown, leaving loved ones, and losing control.

Whenever someone's life expectations are altered, it requires adjustments in his assumptive world.[3] One patient said this about the fear of dying: "Life is pleasant. Death is peaceful. It's the transition that [is] troublesome."[4]

It is recommended that a hospice team support anyone receiving a terminal diagnosis of six months or less to live.

The first hospice was started in the United States in 1974. Medicare offers a hospice benefit for anyone sixty-five and older. Its objective is to provide quality end-of-life care. Many insurance companies also offer a hospice benefit for younger individuals who receive a terminal diagnosis. To qualify for the hospice benefit a physician must verify that the individual has approximately six months or less to live because of his terminal illness.

The primary mission of hospice is to provide a "good death" by keeping patients physically and emotionally comfortable. The roots of the hospice movement are spiritual. Dame Cicely Saunders established hospice after watching the spiritual yearnings that preceded the death of one of her patients, who also became a close friend. Ultimately she decided that she could have more influence with end-of-life care by becoming a physician rather than staying at the bedside as a nurse. Her mission statement for hospice care states: "You matter to the last moment of your life, and we will do all we can, not only to help you die peacefully, but to live until you die."[5]

Families may feel they need to choose aggressive medical treatments for their loved one; however, sometimes less is better. We may have to focus on comfort measures until death comes. Once the patient and the family realize that all has been done to preserve life medically, then comfort may mean stopping aggressive treatments and going home to pass away peacefully.

A mother of a young child who died of cancer wrote,

> My son relapsed after the bone marrow transplant. We were told that all that could be done had been done. I felt such guilt for what I had put him through all these months. There were blood tests, bone marrow aspirations, spinal taps, radiation and chemotherapy that made him so sick. I was with him through them all. They were difficult to watch. Now after all he's been through, it didn't work anyway, I am angry, nervous, uneasy and totally devastated.[6]

Hospice teams can also offer individualized support in hospitals and care centers as well as in patients' homes. Physicians trained in end-of-life care who are experts on pain and symptoms management, oversee the care. Registered nurses administer the best symptom management medications available to control everything from pain and nausea to anxiety. Hospice social workers offer counseling, provide help with life review, and discuss relationship issues with patients and their families. These skilled social workers are especially helpful in offering support to the often conflicted and diverse family members. Hospice aides are available to bathe and dress your loved one while also attending to other personal cares. Hospice chaplains will explore the patient's deepest thoughts and fears and offer spiritual support and prayers while guiding patients and their loved ones through important end-of-life tasks. Hospice also offers bereavement support (after death follow-up care) for the grieving family members.

At least 55 percent of those dying desire someone with whom they can share their fears and concerns.[7] Patients often share personal concerns with hospice team members when they are reluctant to burden or worry their family members. It is sometimes easier for patients to share troubling issues and concerns with a caring professional they feel will not judge them.

Some patients may fear choking, pain, or dying from air hunger. Hospice team members assure the dying that the hospice staff are experts in comfort care and can successfully treat these uncomfortable symptoms. In fact, most deaths come as a gradual slipping away. Some say this is like losing their loved one bit by bit. It is interesting that 54 percent of the patients prefer not being alone, 47 percent want someone to hold their hand, and 50 percent want to either have the opportunity to pray alone or have someone pray for them.[8]

A patient's decline becomes especially evident as their appetite begins to diminish. Patients struggle as it becomes progressively more difficult to eat, and food begins to lose its flavor. As the body slows down, food makes the dying feel bloated and nauseated. As they drink less and become dehydrated, the body produces a natural tranquilizer allowing them to feel comfortable. They may sleep more, withdraw from the world, and turn inward.

Some families try to change these natural dying processes by force-feeding their loved one or by holding back medications to keep them more alert. Unfortunately force-feedings and limiting medications can increase the patient's nausea, vomiting, and diarrhea, which results in unnecessary physical and emotional pain. Families and patients generally do better if they can find meaning in death and accept the natural processes of decline. We should assume that even when the patient can no longer talk to us that he can still feel our gentle touch and hear our soft, loving words.

It is helpful to understand the physical changes that occur as the sick go into what is called the active phase of dying. This can last from hours to days. As the body slows and eventually shuts down, we see more sleeping; less eating; less drinking; and, gradually, more labored breathing. You can swab their mouth, but forcing fluids orally when someone can't swallow can cause choking, aspiration, and other uncomfortable symptoms. It is natural for the muscles and tissues in the throat to relax and for mucus to form. This will cause a noisy, rattled sound as patients breathe. Research reports that it is not uncomfortable to the patient, just to the family hearing the disturbing sounds. Suctioning is uncomfortable; however, sometimes medications or repositioning the patient can soften the sound. The lips, hands, and feet often become cold and bluish in color, and a fever might surface.

As patients near death it is not uncommon for them to reach out to or call the names of deceased loved ones. They talk symbolically about needing to catch a plane, find a key, or get dressed to go somewhere. Assuring them that we will help them get ready and find their way is often comforting.

Some families do better than others. Their strengths and qualities as well as their inadequacies will usually present themselves as they care for their loved one. Family members may not agree with each other on how to care for the dying loved one. They may even be upset with the patient's decision to stop further aggressive medical interventions and treatments. Hospice staff try to honor the patient's wishes relative to their personal treatment. When hospice staff walk into a patient's home or room, the staff put themselves away and focus on the needs and wants of the patient, and then the family. Hospice staff may find patients and families experiencing peace, frustration, grief, anger, gratitude, or a combination of many emotions.[9]

A common scenario happens with married couples when one of them is experiencing a chronic illness and poor health that has extended over many years. The healthy spouse has been in the supporting role as a caregiver when, suddenly, the healthy spouse is diagnosed with a terminal illness. This is a shocking turn of events for the couple, since both assumed that the chronically ill spouse would die first. The tables are turned and the chronically ill spouse is caring for the dying spouse. The dying spouse may feel guilty for now needing care and further burdening his already fatigued and ill spouse. He may also feel guilty for abandoning the chronically ill spouse in anticipation of his own upcoming death.

It is difficult for families to hold on and let go simultaneously. This happens when family members get ready for the death of their loved one, only to have him go into remission and his life span extended. It is natural to think the caregiver would be thrilled with more time together. However, often the enormous emotional energy necessary to detach can be so painful that the task of reattaching seems unbearable. The patient becomes confused as well and at times feels everyone has already given up and buried him.

I have often heard people say that we die how we've lived. If someone is social, he may want people around and involved as he passes on. The private individual may approach death in a more isolated fashion. Some are accepting of their fate while others go out kicking and screaming. A hospice staff's goal is to help patients die the way they choose.

Woody Allen put it well when he said, "I'm not afraid to die. I just don't want to be there when it happens!"[10]

The truth is that some of us are very afraid to die. We may fear choking and difficulty with breathing. Some fear leaving loved ones and facing the unknowns or God's judgment.

There are processes families and patients can implement to help enhance a peaceful death, or a good death. Some helpful end-of-life tasks and processes include the following:

1. Acknowledging our regrets and saying "I'm sorry."

No one is or has been a perfect child, spouse, or parent. We have all done or said something that we wished we hadn't. It can be healing to openly talk about these issues and put them behind us.

2. Acknowledging that others make mistakes, and then being willing to forgive them. We can follow the Savior's example by offering forgiveness to family or others who may have hurt us. "Father, forgive them; for they know not what they do" (Luke 23:34).

3. Saying "I love you." "A new commandment I give unto you, That ye love one another; as I have loved you, that ye also love one another" (John 13:34).

4. Remembering. It is valuable to talk about our life memories. This is called life review. It is an important end-of-life task. It keeps the dying's self-esteem intact by remembering who they are and what they have accomplished. This can be done by looking at scrapbooks together, or creating them.

5. Saying good-bye. Saying the final good-bye can be a difficult end-of-life task to perform. We often remind families they can do it every time they say good night. It could go something like this: "I hope I see you tomorrow. If not, know that I love you, Dad.

I will really miss you, but I will take care of Mom and carry on in your name."

6. Unfinished business. We're referring to financial and other personal affairs as well as resolving unfinished personal issues. Doing so will put both the patient and his family at ease so they won't have to worry that his death will cause unnecessary burdens for those left behind.

Hospice staff try to help families understand that their loved one has a good chance of dying alone. It may happen when the caregiver goes to the mailbox, grabs a bite to eat, or falls asleep. "When the loyal guard leaves, so does the soul from the body of the guarded."[11]

They also help families understand that "preparing for Death is one of the most profoundly healing acts of a lifetime."[12]

Many individuals with a terminal illness will ask, "Is it my time to go?" The Lord has told us that the sick will be healed if there is sufficient faith and if the person "is not appointed unto death" (Doctrine and Covenants 42:48). Acts 17:26 says there is a determined time and appointed habitation. Hebrews 9:27, Job 14:14, and Alma 42:6 talk about being appointed to death. It was a comfort to many at Richard L. Evans's funeral when President Joseph Fielding Smith said, "No righteous man is ever taken before his time."[13]

Others dying have reported that during their near-death

accounts they were told it was not their time to die and they had to return to earth. Some were even given a choice to stay or return. Recently, a hospice patient shared a near-death experience he had a few years previously. After a surgical procedure, he found himself out of his body, viewing it from above. Soon he was joined by a personage in white who reminded him of what he thought Moses might look like. He was told that he must go back into his body because it was not his time to die.

Many dying patients seem to hang on, waiting for a specific time to die. It may be a child's graduation, a loved one's wedding, the coming season, or a special holiday. It sometimes involves the completion of some important endeavor they have worked for. A few years ago, on Easter weekend, three of our hospice patients died on Good Friday, three more on Saturday, and three more on Easter Sunday. I've seen others who seem to wait until someone who is traveling to see them arrives. It's important for them to say their good-byes and have closure. Some seem to hold on to life, hoping to make peace with someone they had experienced relationship problems with in the past.

The Lord may also intervene and extend life. See Helaman 15:4, 10–11 where the Lord "prolonged their days." Alma 9:16 indicates that "the Lord will . . . prolong their existence in the land," and Doctrine and Covenants 5:33 promises "that thy days may be prolonged."

President Kimball said: "I am grateful that even through the priesthood I cannot heal all the sick. I might heal people who should die. I might relieve people of suffering who should suffer. I fear I would frustrate the purpose of God."[14]

He also asked, "What if we did have power to heal? Would we have allowed Abinadi to die in the flames of fire?" Abinadi said, "Touch me not, for God shall smite you . . . for I have not delivered the message which the Lord sent me to deliver . . . therefore, God will not suffer that I shall be destroyed at this time. . . . Ye see that ye have not power to slay me" (Mosiah 13:3, 7).

After Abinadi delivered his message and was martyred, he prayed, "O God, receive my soul" (Mosiah 17:19).

At-Death Experiences (ADEs)

At-death experiences (ADEs) have brought spiritual healing to those observing the event as well as to those dying. Some dying nonbelievers say that they have seen angels or deceased relatives just prior to their deaths. These experiences often convert them to the reality that there is life beyond death.

One interesting story involved a dying woman's ADE. She was anticipating joining her husband who had died some years before. One day she experienced an ADE that had left her puzzled. She asked one of the hospice nurses, "Why is my sister with my deceased husband?" The hospice worker talked with one of the other family members. She asked if the sister was dead. She was told that her sister was in China and had died just a couple of days before. The family had decided not to tell their mother for fear it would upset her. They then decided to tell her about her sister's death because they realized it would give her spiritual comfort and make sense in light of her vision as she herself faced death.[15]

One dying woman awoke with a beautiful smile on her face as she reached for something unseen. She seemed to put her arms together in a cradling position as she looked lovingly into her arms. As her family discussed this event, they realized that her first baby had died just moments after birth. She later had other children and the fact that she had lost a child was hardly ever discussed. This realization was a sweet moment for her family as they concluded that as she died, their mother was allowed to see and hold her deceased spirit baby.[16]

When someone is dying, it is important that we pay attention to everything they say and do because their communications may be subtle and symbolic. We could miss some of these last communications because of our own preoccupations. Sometimes the important messages shared will be vague and confusing. Those present may think that the dying person is delirious or confused rather than trying to communicate something important. Common events occurring prior to death include dying individuals staring through you as if to see something else. In other instances they may seem distracted or offer inappropriate smiles or gestures, pointing or reaching for something unseen, and sometimes calling out names.

They may report hearing voices. It is not usually helpful to argue or challenge what the dying are seeing or otherwise sensing.

I was working in the hospital the same day that my paternal grandmother was brought in with heart palpitations. I went to her room on my break to feed her dinner. She visited with me and ate a little. At the end of our visit she looked off into the corner of the room and called out my deceased grandfather's name. We then discussed how she had missed him for the last ten years and how she was looking forward to being with him again. She died a few hours later.

Some dying individuals talk about getting ready to go on a trip. For example, a pilot talked about getting ready to go on a flight. It might be helpful to go along with the symbolism and ask questions such as, "Do you know when it leaves?" and "Can I help you get ready?" If we try to relate to the dying person's world, it can help him experience a more meaningful and peaceful death. If we have trouble understanding, it is okay to say, "I think you are trying to tell me something important and I am trying very hard to understand, but I am just not getting it. Please keep trying to tell me."

One man described missing his trolley. A wise hospice nurse told him that she was sure that the trolley would stop for him soon and that he would be able to get on. The trolley was his symbolic way of saying, "It is time for me to go." It wasn't long after that he died.[17]

Recently I was visiting a hospice patient that we had served for several months. The past month she rarely communicated with her family or our staff. This particular visit I asked how she was. She said, "Not well; I've had a terrible crash." I asked her if she thought she was dying. She nodded her head yes. I asked her if she was ready to go. Again she nodded yes. I asked her if she was afraid and she shook her head no. We shared some other special symbolic communication, and she died a couple of days later.

Many will describe seeing a beautiful place. If they do, it is okay to say, "I'm happy that you see such a beautiful place and that it makes you happy." Others may reluctantly share their fears. It is important to address any concerns: past regrets, strained relationships, unfinished business, a need for repentance, and so forth. Encourage the dying by telling them you want to understand what they are saying. You might ask them, "Can you tell me more?" Pace yourself and don't push them. Let the dying control the conversation.

It has also been helpful to believe those who die are no longer suffering because they are in a beautiful afterworld. It is those of us left behind that struggle through the loss and grief issues. President Kimball reminds us that the Lord does not usually view death as a curse or a tragedy.[18]

The following scripture can also give us comfort: "Blessed are the dead that die in the Lord" (Doctrine and Covenants 63:49).

Because of the veil over our eyes and our limited understanding, it is sometimes hard to realize the Lord's promise that "those that die in me shall not taste of death, for it shall be sweet unto them" (Doctrine and Covenants 42:46).

However, the Lord realizes the pain we experience losing our loved ones. He makes us the following promise about the Millennium and our next life: "There shall be no sorrow because there is no death" (Doctrine and Covenants 101:29).

"And God shall wipe away all tears from their eyes; and there shall be no more death, neither sorrow, nor crying, neither shall there be any more pain: for the former things are passed away" (Revelation 21:4).

He also counsels us to "weep for the loss of them that die, and more especially for those that have not hope of a glorious resurrection" (Doctrine and Covenants 42:45).

He has left us the Comforter and promises, "blessed are all they that mourn, for they shall be comforted" (3 Nephi 12:4; see also Matthew 5:4).

Notes

1. *Cancer Facts & Figures* (Atlanta: American Cancer Society, 1998).
2. Gallup telephone Poll, 1997. National sample of 1200.
3. T. A. Rando (speech, Association for Death Education and Counseling Conference, Chicago, March 1998).
4. Isaac Asimov, http://en.wikiquote.org/wiki/Isaac_Asimov (accessed September 10, 2008).

5. Dame Cicely Saunder, http://mercatornet.com/articles (accessed July 30, 2005).
6. T. A. Rando, ed. *Clinical Dimensions of Anticipatory Mourning: Theory and Practice in Working with the Dying, Their Loved Ones, and Their Caregivers* (Champaign, Illinois: Research Press, 2000), 7.
7. Gallup telephone Poll, 1997. National sample of 1200.
8. Ibid.
9. Kit Jackson (speech, Utah Hospice Palliative Care Organization, Davis Conference Center, Layton, Utah, November 9, 2005).
10. Woody Allen, http://www.brainquote.com (accessed September 10, 2008).
11. Neale Donald Walsh, *Conversations with God: An Uncommon Dialogue*, Book 1, (New York: G. P. Putnam's Sons, 1995) , 80.
12. Stephen Levine, *A Year to Live* (New York: Bell Tower, 1997), 7.
13. Smith, "Funeral Services for Richard L. Evans," *Ensign*, December 1971, 10.
14. Spencer W. Kimball, *Faith Precedes the Miracle* (Salt Lake City: Deseret Book, 1979), 99.
15. M. Callanan & P. Kelley, *Final Gifts* (New York: Bantom Books, 1992), 92–93.
16. Ibid., 179
17. Ibid., chapter 6
18. Kimball, *Faith Precedes the Miracle*, 101

CHAPTER THREE

Death of a Loved One

AS MY MOTHER'S MEMORY SLOWLY DECLINED OVER THE YEARS, I wanted her to experience one more trip to the early Church historic sites that she loved. We traveled to Winter Quarters in Omaha, Nebraska, to visit the pioneer sites and monuments there. I was especially interested in the Winter Quarters memorial statue that stands in the cemetery behind the Winter Quarters Temple. I had only seen pictures and smaller replicas of this life-sized pioneer statue that was dedicated in 1936. The statue depicts a pioneer man and woman huddled together with a shovel in hand. They are looking down sadly on a grave they have just dug for a deceased loved one. As I gazed on this beautiful statue, I asked my mother to take a picture of me standing close to the grieving couple. As I got up to the statue for the photo, I looked down and discovered that the artist, Avard Fairbanks, had chosen to sculpt a small child lying on its back in an open grave. I was overcome with emotion as I felt witness to the intense grief and suffering these pioneer parents had to endure.

It was Dennis that had first noticed the backside of this same statue a few years earlier while attending a training seminar for LDS Family Services. He came home and described the large roots coming out of the ground that are attached to the legs and backs of the pioneer couple. It looked to us as if these roots could pull them down and bury them in the ground as well. This symbolism of grief and mourning had a profound effect on both of us since we have buried two of our own children.

Although both of us work with grieving individuals, we were shocked at our own pain and suffering following our personal losses. We had learned much through our study of loss and grief, but we hadn't felt the deep suffering of the heart until we experienced it first hand. We were surprised that research has shown that it can take many months or years to adjust and find one's "new normal."[1]

We wouldn't have believed the time frame if we had not experienced grief firsthand. We realized, as many others have, that we never can be the same following a significant loss. Our loss and all that we have since experienced are now becoming part of our new normal. As our priorities change, we see through new eyes. Finding our new normal usually takes longer than we expect or would like. After losing Joseph with his coat of many colors, Jacob refused to be comforted and said, "For I will go down into the grave unto my son mourning" (Genesis 37:35). I recently heard a mother whose daughter had been murdered express similar feelings, followed by her own reassurance that we can find comfort in knowing where our loved ones are. It is helpful to realize that faith and grief are both uniquely important but separate principles. Each requires actions on our part to fully benefit and sustain us in times of loss. We will always miss and grieve the earthly presence of our loved ones, even when knowing where they are.

The death of a loved one is an experience that most of us will face someday. When that moment comes, we may discover the poignant reality expressed so well in the movie, *Man's Search for Happiness*. "Life's greatest test comes with the death of a loved one, and without faith in the immortality of the soul, the separation of death looms forever comfortless."[2]

In this chapter we hope to give you helpful information as you exercise faith and receive the necessary comfort to survive your loss.

We all experience different types of grief, mourning as we confront different types of death. The death of a parent is considered a loss of our past while the death of a spouse constitutes the loss of our present. The death of a child (often the most challenging) represents the loss of the hopes and dreams for our future.

Loss of a Spouse

Although some professionals feel there is more social understanding and support with the loss of a spouse, losing one's best friend, lover, and life companion leaves many profoundly lonely. Even when we realize that one of us must go first, it is no easy task. We often experience a loss of identity. We were once a married couple and now we are a widow or widower. We may not like the label or the feeling of being alone in the world.

Widowers usually display less emotional grief and have more trouble adapting to the practical problems, like housework and child care. Widows usually experience a sense of abandonment and may require more help with emotional issues. The most common complaint expressed by both is the loneliness felt following the loss of a spouse.

One woman said after the death of her husband, "It is so hard. I need help. I am falling apart. I am not coping. I don't know what to do."

Another widow was asked by friends, "What can we do to help you?" Her reply was, "Undo it!"

A man who lost his wife said, "My wife was so healthy when she suddenly got ill and died. I am still in shock to be left alone so suddenly. I go over and over the details of her death. I am so emotional."

We often struggle to understand the impact of someone else's loss. In our attempt to provide encouragement, we often say the wrong things. A sister in one of our wards lost her husband and son in the same accident. The Relief Society president said to her, "Well, some people lose their whole family. At least you have your daughter." This mother was angered by the statement and went inactive for years. She turned her anger toward the Church because a well-meaning member and Church representative made a hurtful statement. (See *But If Not, Volume I*, for more information on spiritual injury.)

Another widow who had cared for her ill husband for many years was told, "You should be glad, now you can have a life."

Many don't understand that caring for someone so intensely often deepens our bond with them, thus complicating or intensifying our loss. It's also normal to feel relief from the hard work of caring for a loved one and watching them suffer; however, most will still mourn and miss them.

Death of a Parent

Over twelve million Americans will bury a parent this year. Unfortunately, the grief of adult children is often disenfranchised (overlooked). Because society expects, accepts, and discounts the loss of older parents, their children's grief consequently goes unrecognized. In reality, the death of a parent can be difficult at any age.

Young children often struggle as they attempt to make sense

of a loss they can't developmentally understand. In addition, some children experience a sense of abandonment after the death of a parent, which may cause anxiety and depression.

A young girl who lost her mother stated, "I know that I should be happy. She's well in heaven. But I miss her so!"

What relief she felt when she learned it was okay and normal to miss her mother and feel sad. She, like many, needed permission to grieve.

A twenty-one-year-old woman said, "My mother died after years of suffering. I felt relieved that her suffering had ended."

My own mother's parents died when she was fourteen. She told us that she would often go in her parents coat closet and put on her mother's fur coat and weep. She felt comfort by cuddling herself in the coat. The smell and warmth allowed her to feel close to her mother, both physically and spiritually.

I couldn't sleep well for two weeks after my father died. We had traveled many miles to be with him on Christmas Day. He died early that Christmas morning. I couldn't understand how my mother could sleep in the bed where he died that very night. I could hardly walk past the bedroom. It was frightening for me because his bed was where Dennis, my brother, and I performed CPR to keep him alive until the paramedics arrived.

Now, twenty years later, Mother (Vivian Johnson Marsden) died just a few months before the printing of this volume. She had the perfect death or a "good death" as we call it in hospice.

She was eighty-two years old, living alone, and caring for herself until her cancer diagnosis six months earlier. She had five children, their spouses, and grandchildren who helped keep her at home as long as possible. She experienced a little dementia, which was a blessing because she never realized how sick she really was. As she declined, the family gave Dennis and me permission to care for her at our home with the support of Rocky Mountain Hospice. She lived comfortably for three months, surrounded and supported by her five children, their spouses, and grandchildren. She was a spiritual saint, choosing to be an "instrument in God's hands," as my brother put it. She was a Relief Society stake and ward president for over fifteen years. She served three full-time missions and continued to serve as a ward missionary until four months prior to her passing.

We had just finished watching the first session of general conference when Dennis and I thought her eyes looked different. She hadn't been eating or drinking much for a few days. I went and looked at the calendar to confirm the date—April 6, of course! I thought if she could pick her day to die this would be it. She loved the Restoration of the gospel and she never missed a session of general conference, including this one. (She had often told us that she thought dad dying on Christmas was a special day for someone to meet the Savior.)

I called my brother and asked if he could come after conference and give her a blessing. I was hoping it would be a blessing of release, if my brother was inspired to do so. After the closing prayer, we gathered around her bed as a family. At the end of her beautiful blessing, my brother asked, "When did she start breathing like that?" I replied, "As soon as you said amen." She took a few quiet, peaceful breaths and was gone. We all sat in silence and basked in the spirit. Dennis said, "I haven't witnessed many miracles in my life, but I believe we have witnessed a miracle today."

Our youngest daughter got married three weeks later and our youngest son moved out of state for medical school. Our house feels empty now. We miss the three of them living in our home. We are again experiencing loss and grief.

We are also experiencing a new phenomenon, one that has been described to us by our clients, but now we sense it ourselves and understand it more clearly. Having buried our grandparents and all four parents, we are suddenly the "old" generation. We are truly the grandparents, the ones who will die next. For the first time, we see, feel, and fear our own death and mortality. It is lonelier than we expected and more frightening than we imagined. This, like all of life's losses and changes, will require grief work and faith to adjust and find meaning.

Loss of a Sibling

Loss of a sibling can be very confusing for young children as well as adult survivors. It is common for the bereaved to canonize the deceased. It is also common for other siblings to feel unloved, or think that their parents love the deceased sibling more. One child said, "My mother kept saying the joy of her life was gone after my brother died."

Well-meaning comments can also cause pain and damage relationships. A female acquaintance of ours said, "Soon after my brother died, my visiting teacher kept asking if and when my sister-in-law would remarry. This upset me and really hurt my feelings."

Some lack the ability to fully express their feelings. A sibling writes, "When my parents start getting down about the death of my brother, I usually leave the room. I just can't talk to them about him. I don't know how to talk to them. I feel like no matter what I say it comes out wrong and hurts them. I'm not good at saying what I mean. I'm afraid to cry about the death of my brother because it might upset them more. I cry alone most of the time. I can talk to my sister."

After Cameron died, one of our sons shared, "I feel guilty that I hadn't been a better brother. I should have been kinder to him."

Children and Loss:

A child's abnormal, bad behaviors or rebelliousness may be a way of acting out his or her pain and grief. Grief and loss can be confusing for children. They may become angry at God or the Church because they feel God should have prevented their tragedy or protected their loved one. Spiritual injury may result when a child's prayer isn't answered how they hoped it would be. Many young children have earnestly prayed for a loved one to recover, only to watch them eventually die.

Parents should encourage (not pressure) children to express their feelings and fears by allowing them to be active participants in coping with the crisis, illness, or death. Children can usually sense increased stress and anxiety in the home. They may feel and recognize that something is not right. If children are not told honestly or allowed to share in what is happening, they may become confused, frightened, and insecure. They feel secure when parents share their feelings openly and regularly. They may also feel comfort and reassurance when parents share personal testimony, read scriptures, and pray with them.

Family home evenings can be a forum for family sharing and listening. Children should also be involved in the open acknowledgment of family issues and problem solving. Including them in challenges doesn't mean parents should overwhelm them with their own grief, guilt, and unrealistic expectations. Children cannot fully comprehend a parent's pain. They have developmental limitations based on their age and limited life experience. They often remember and regrieve certain aspects of their loss as they grow and mature. They may experience a loss of trust toward their parents if important issues affecting the family are kept from them.

Children look to adults, especially their parents as examples of how to respond to life events. Seeing and sharing our grief and disappointments in healthy ways often validates a child's own sadness, confusion, or other emotions. It's a challenging and sobering responsibility to acknowledge that, "Parents can complicate or facilitate the grief process for children."[3]

A five-year-old was confused with her mother's fluctuating behavior and mood. She would see tears in her mother's eyes and ask, "Why are you sad mommy?" Her mother would reply that she was just tired because she was pregnant. What she didn't share was that she was carrying twins and knew one of the twins would not live due to a serious birth defect.

This went on for a couple of months. A few days before the delivery, their doctor hoped that some reading material and encouraging a more open communication style might help the family.

After reading some grief literature, the mom told her daughter that two baby girls would be born, but that they could only bring home one sister because the other was sick and wouldn't live very long. This curious child asked many questions. When she got the answers she needed, she returned to her play.

When the babies were born, the child was allowed to see, hold, and kiss both babies. The baby with the birth defect died a few hours later. As this five-year-old saw her parents and grandparents cry, she asked additional questions. When she had sufficient contact with both of her baby sisters, she turned her focus back to her crayons and dolls.

The entire family spent time with the deceased baby sister. They had said a brief hello and now had to say good-bye. With time, everyone seemed to adjust to the loss, including the five-year-old.

It has been said that, "Children can't tolerate intense emotions for very long. Children generally have a short feeling phase."[4]

After his brother's death, our seven-year-old son Brandon wondered, "Am I crying enough?" However, he was unable or unwilling to verbalize this guilt until he was fifteen years old. At age sixteen, he wrote a poem about an ornamental pear tree we planted eight years earlier in Cameron's memory. We were surprised at the deep feelings and understanding that he could now express.

The Pear Tree

Death, the disabled brother gone
Crippled, but much stronger than us all
Sadness and grief of the loss
Of a great brother, son, and example
Now planted in the earth his body lies
A small sapling also then planted
Small and weak, could barely stand
Weak as he once was
Year after year it grows
Stronger and taller it points to the sky
A remembrance of joys
That still live on
Beautiful, soft, white, flowers

Blooming on his day of birth
Falling to the earth
The month of his passing
The memorial Pear Tree
A true symbol of Cameron
Standing tall and firm above us
As he is now, while he watches below

In young children, we may see bedwetting, returning to the bottle, clinging, and phobias. Encouraging open communication may aid in the healing process. Remember, young children communicate in many ways. Some may communicate subtly through behaviors and play. Others may communicate through art and music. Young boys often grieve through anger, while many girls become caregivers. We can help children become healthy survivors, rather than victims, by offering support. We can guide children toward letting go of unrealistic blame and rechanneling their energies into meaningful and productive tasks.

The following are age characteristics of grieving children.

Two and Under

These children react behaviorally to stresses around them. They can sense tension in the home and conflicts between their parents. They may react by crying, or through changes in behaviors such as eating, sleeping, bathroom habits, withdrawing, or temper tantrums. They respond best to consistent nurturing from significant others in their lives.

Three- to Five-Year-Olds

These children often react with similar behavior changes as those two and under. In addition, they may be very curious, asking many questions. Answer as simply and honestly as possible. We may see their grief as they color, draw, sing, or play. Many children act out parts of the crisis with dolls and toys as they play house. They may also respond like six- to nine-year-olds, feeling guilty that somehow they caused the crisis. We should allow them to talk and give them extra attention and hugs.

Six- to Nine-Year-Olds

Generally they can understand adversity, illness, and death. They recognize that death is final. They may feel that bad thoughts, wishes, or anger they experienced in the past caused the illness or death. They need hope for a positive future. They may experience negative dreams. We may see them acting out their loss issues through behavior problems or poor academic performance. Their physical symptoms can be similar to teens and adults. They need reassurance and reminders that others love them.

Ten- to Twelve-Year-Olds

They may want more answers about what happened and why. They may kid or joke about illness or death to hide their true fears and anxieties. Provide honest answers to their specific questions, allowing them to set the pace of the discussion.

Adolescents

Adolescents can react as an adult would, with confusion, withdrawal, depression, or intense emotions. However, because of their preoccupation with self, they may not feel the same depth of grief experienced by adults. Their recovery is often more rapid than adults.

After Cam's death, our teenage son reported, "After my brother died, I was afraid to talk to my parents. I decided to go back into the family room where my parents were. I remember sitting on the couch, listening to my parents cry. I didn't cry, I just sat there staring at the balloons that said, 'Get well Soon!' A couple of days later at the funeral, it all got worse. I became more angry and depressed."

Although teens understand death is final for others, they often personally feel immortal. Consequently they may still participate in risk-taking activities as they search for their own personal identity.

Adolescents are often self-focused, which takes most of their time and energy. They are also preoccupied with friends and need our love and support to become free of peer pressure. They are concerned with day-to-day events, and may want to hurry through the grieving process and get their lives back to normal.

We should avoid telling teens how they should feel or react. Lecturing, comparing, or overcontrolling doesn't usually work.

They need good role models, encouragement, and a listening ear at crucial moments. It is often after midnight!

Loss of a Child

"The death of a child is like no other. Parents experience the symptoms of grief more intensely and far longer than with any other loss."[5] For many years, Dennis and I worked with parents who had lost children. However, we hadn't fully realized that their suffering and pain was so intense until we lost two of our own. We were shocked at the magnitude of our own grief. We discovered that it can be difficult to understand what someone else is going through until we experience it ourselves. The following excerpts are from parents in a support group who have lost a child.

One person said, "I can still feel today the absolute cold feeling of my son's skin as I kissed him good-bye on the forehead. That will be with me forever as a reminder that he was taken from us so suddenly, and represents the feeling of absence and loss that weigh upon us."

A father lamented, "I miss watching her jump on the trampoline. She always wanted me to spot her. I also miss my old life and how my wife was before this tragedy. We can never be the same."

John Craig, a family therapist, lost two daughters, fourteen and sixteen, in a car-train accident. A few years later, another daughter died of meningitis. He said:

For me, the night our two daughters died changed everything. I would never be the same, feel the same, or be completely at ease again. And more significantly, neither would the rest of my family. My grief began with outrage. How could God or life be so contemptuous of me? What possible wrong could I have committed that would bring such ruthless destruction to my family? It hit me with a blunt force hard enough that even after eighteen years, I still experience an ache that threatens to undo me, to expel me from among the faithful. Yet I have not yet given in to the demon of discouragement or succumbed to spiritual death—not even when six years later that awful monster, death (2 Nephi 9:10), came again to my home. This time it was my middle daughter taken in one day from the blush of health to the darkness of the grave.

Through yet another siege of overwhelming sadness, way beyond my ability to endure, I remained confused, disoriented, and perpetually dissatisfied with my life, but I didn't and haven't quit. Instead I reach for the Comforter; I pray for peace nightly, and I take heart in the promises extended by the Savior of the World.[6]

A friend of mine said, "It has been almost twenty years since the car accident of our three-year-old son. I know I will be with him in the celestial kingdom; however, I still miss him and wish I could have raised him on earth. Our grief was very intense at first. It almost cost us our marriage. Our grief has turned into mourning, which seems to be staying with us a lifetime."

Hyrum G. Smith said the following:

There are many of our Latter-day Saint mothers who have

mourned the loss of their little children, and many mothers have felt that they themselves had committed some great sin, else their little ones would not be taken from them. Now, to such mothers let me say, do not accuse the Lord of taking your little ones from you, nor feel that you have committed any great sin, that those little ones are taken from you, because the Lord loves little children and he will not treat them unkindly, nor without mercy, for through the blood of his atonement they shall come forth in the morning of the Resurrection with his Saints, and they shall be glorified according to the works they would have accomplished in the earth had they lived."[7]

Professionals are now suggesting that, "Accommodation in contrast to recovery captures more accurately the process that most individuals experience following a major loss. Major losses can be integrated into the rest of life; however, final closure after the death of a loved one usually cannot be obtained and is not even desirable."[8]

An example of this reality is evident in the account of a mother whose child died forty years ago. She recently ran into her deceased daughter's best friend who was shopping with her granddaughter. This mother experienced a grief attack. She mourned again as she realized that she had missed forty years without her daughter and was now also missing her role as grandmother and great-grandmother to lost generations of grandchildren! This account illustrates the developmental aspects of her grief.

A Time to Die?

Typical questions asked by those who lose a loved one are: Does everyone have a specific time assigned to leave earth life? What does appointed time mean? Is it a specific day, month, or year? What about those who die of sudden accidents? What about those who die as the result of murder?

Ecclesiastes 3:1–2 tells us, "To everything there is a season, and a time to every purpose under the heaven: a time to be born and a time to die; a time to plant, and a time pluck up that which is planted."

President Spencer W. Kimball taught that we can die prematurely when he said, "I am confident that there is a time to die. I am not a fatalist. I believe that many people die before their time be-cause they are careless, abuse their bodies, take unnecessary chances, or expose themselves to hazard, accident, and sickness."[9]

Lehi and Nephi, the Sons of Helaman, were protected by God. They were put into prison without food. Their persecutors tried to slay them, but could not. They were encircled about as if by fire, and they said, "Ye cannot lay your hands on us to slay us" (Helaman 5:26, 29).

Christ sensed when it was his time to die. He said, "Mine hour is not come" (John 2:4, 7:30). As his martyrdom drew closer, he announced to His disciples, "The hour is come" (John 12:23) and "It is finished" (John 19:30).

Elder Neal A. Maxwell wrote, "God is never surprised by unexpected arrivals in the spirit world . . . we must always distinguish between God's being able to foresee and His causing or desiring something to happen."[10]

Grieving Variables

Some may use the word recovery as they describe the grief process. However, better words may be that we will reconcile, adapt, or adjust to our loss of a loved one. How we ultimately grieve and cope is as individual as each of our thumbprints.

There are many variables that account for how someone will experience the death of a loved one. Who died, and how close was I to this person? Often, the depth of our love, time, and emotional investments coincide with the depth of our grief. Was the death an expected loss, possibly of an elderly loved one who was at peace and ready to go? I have seen this kind of death with my hospice work and it can be a beautiful experience. We may feel relief that their suffering is over. However, one of my saddest and loneliest patients was a ninety-six-year-old husband who wanted his ninety-eight-year-old wife to just live a few more years.

Heber J. Grant expressed shock and grief when his mother, who was in her eighties and was his best friend, died before reaching one hundred as he had expected.

Another factor in how we may experience grief relates to the amount of time one has to prepare for the death and to say good-bye. We knew our ninety-year-old grandmother was dying and we were able to help her do some end-of-life tasks, express our love, and say good-bye. When my fairly young father died suddenly of heart disease and Dennis's mother took her own life at age fifty, we weren't able to express these heartfelt messages. We had to do these end-of-life tasks vicariously with our deceased son and parents who died suddenly. (It can be done through writing down our thoughts in a letter to our deceased loved ones or talking out loud to them in an "empty chair.")

There are also differences between a sudden death and an anticipated death. Anticipated death is like standing on a street corner as you see someone running toward you. Soon they are upon you, knocking you down as they continue running away; you saw them coming and you knew what hit you. In sudden death, your back was turned and you didn't see the runner coming; you didn't have time to brace yourself. Suddenly, you find yourself flat on the ground with no idea of what hit you. It will take longer for the brain to adjust, and for the shock to soften after experiencing unexpected death.[11]

Paradigm Shift

We need not fear the future; we can still find joy, peace, and happiness again. To achieve future peace, we might consider what Steven Covey calls a paradigm shift. In a paradigm shift, we come to view and define the meaning associated with the same event dramatically differently. An example of looking at an event from another angle became clear to us when we were driving to the mortuary to see our deceased son in his casket for the first time. Dennis found himself sitting through a red light and still didn't move when it turned green. He was moving in slow motion still in shock from Cameron's sudden death the night before. The man behind him started honking, raising his fists, and yelling at Dennis. Most likely, if the angry driver had known where we were going and why Dennis wasn't moving, he would have shifted the way he looked at the event and remained patient. There would be a predictable change in his response if he also had a young child, and a guaranteed shift in his paradigm if he had buried one.

Another example of a paradigm shift occurred when my father died on Christmas. While we were waiting for the ambulance I would go in another room and ask the Lord to let my father live, especially since it was Christmas. My prayer was not answered how I thought it should be. However, my mother helped me reconstruct my view and the thoughts that were upsetting to me. She shared that she felt Christmas was a special day to go to the spirit world and meet the Savior.

Loss of Identity

For a time after the death of a loved one it may be hard to interact with others. We may feel wounded, devastated, and vulnerable. Some withdraw and isolate themselves from the very support they so desperately need. We may also feel deserted and experience a loss of identity. We may feel uncomfortable being introduced as a widow or a widower rather than a married couple. President Hinckley described this process when he spoke following the death of wife, Marjorie. "Only those who have passed through this dark valley know of its utter desolation. To lose one's much-loved partner . . . is absolutely devastating."[12]

A loss of identity is also common especially if we were a caregiver and had invested significant time and energy caring for our deceased loved one. I felt very lost for a long time wondering what to do with all the time and energy I had previously spent caring for our disabled child. Some feel they are under glass, continually scrutinized and judged for how or how long they are grieving. Consequently, many wear masks, pretending to be coping well. As they mourn alone in the shadows, they are experiencing disenfranchised grief because they feel like few understand their pain. One woman asked, "What would the ward members think of me if they knew I really wasn't coping well with my husband's death?" To cope with these social symptoms, we encourage our patients to decrease their isolation and try to accept others' support. A daily phone call from family or friends asking how we are doing can help a great deal. Many hospitals and mortuaries now offer bereavement support groups where mourners can talk with others who are grieving similar losses.

Service

Service can be a healing tool. You will increase the likelihood of finding meaning and purpose in your loss as you reach out to others who are also hurting. At the last supper, knowing of His fate, Christ asked His disciples to love one another. When He hung on the cross He looked at His weeping mother and said "Woman, behold thy son," and then looking at John, "Behold thy mother" (John 19:26, 27). He encouraged them to care for and look after one another. He asks the same of us today.

On Cameron's first birthday following his death, we were missing him and feeling sad and depressed. We decided to take a meal to a woman who was confined to her home. After visiting with her, we acknowledged that we both felt better and that our sadness had lifted as we helped another.

We remember our first sacrament meeting after the death of Cameron. We used to watch him proudly pass the sacrament with a silver tray attached to his electric wheelchair. The Sunday following his death there was no wheelchair, no silver tray, and of course, no Cameron. This Sunday void stayed with us for many sacrament meetings. Hospice widows and widowers often share with us that sitting alone after many years of marriage and hearing the familiar hymns which used to bring comfort, now bring a flood of tears and grief.

Loving in Absence:

We miss our son very much. We have had to learn to love him in absence because we can no longer love him in presence.[13] Because someone has died does not mean the love or relationship ends.

We mourn for others who have lost loved ones. We look forward with great anticipation to claim the hope of the Resurrection and see our son again. We draw comfort from the scriptures that say, "Because I live, ye shall live also" (John 14:19) and "Whosoever liveth and believeth in me shall never die" (John 11:26).

For coping tools and grief interventions, see *But If Not, Volume I*.

Notes

1. Rana K. Limbo and Sara Rich Wheeler, *When a Baby Dies: A Handbook for Helping and Healing* (La Crosse Lutheran Hospital/Gunderson Clinic, Ltd., 1986), xv.
2. *Man's Search for Happiness*, original film, directed by Judge Whitaker (Provo, Utah: Brigham Young University, 1964).
3. K. Doka, "Living with Grief" (speech, Hospice Foundation of America National Teleconference, April 14, 1999).
4. A. Wolfelt (speech, Association for Death Education and Counseling Conference, Chicago, March 1998).
5. Barbara E. Rosof, *The Worst Loss: How Families Heal from the Death of a Child* (New York: H. Holt & Co., 1994), 3.
6. Craig, "Surviving the Death of a Child: It Takes Courage to Believe," Essay G5, *Helping and Healing Our Families* (Salt Lake City: Deseret

Book/Brigham Young University, 2005), 280–81.

7. Smith, in Conference Report, April 1917, 70–71.

8. T. A. Rando, "Grieving and Mourning: Accommodating to loss," *Dying: Facing the Facts*, edited by H. Wass and R. A. Niemeyer, (Washington DC: Taylor & Francis, 1995), 221.

9. Kimball, *Faith Precedes the Miracle*, 103.

10. Neil A. Maxwell, *All These Things Shall Give Thee Experience*, (Salt Lake City: Deseret Book, 1979), 18.

11. T. A. Rando (speech, Association for Death Education and Counseling Conference, Chicago, March 1998).

12. Ann Bennion Brown, *The Widow's Might*, (Springville, Utah: Horizon Publishers, 2007), x.

13. T. A. Rando, *Clinical Dimension Of Anticipatory Mourning: Theory and Practice in Working with the Dying, Their Loved Ones, and Their Caregivers* (Champaign, Illinois: Research Press, 2000), 192.

CHAPTER FOUR

Death and Spirituality

SOME SURVIVORS ARE SPIRITUALLY INJURED WHEN they
experience the death of a loved one. Spiritual injury results when
life's realities contradict previously held spiritual assumptions.
The night before our fourteen-year-old's hip surgery, I told him
if anything went wrong I hoped he would come back from the
spirit world to let me know he was okay. As the mother of a
deceased infant and a child with cerebral palsy, I worried and
wanted reassurance. However, the look in Cameron's eyes
caused me to change my request. I said, "If you can't come back,
or shouldn't, don't worry, I will just have faith that you are okay.
He died suddenly and unexpectedly in a close observation room
at twelve midnight, thirty-six hours after his surgery, with a
nurse and Dennis at his side.

Initially I really thought that Cameron would come to visit me. I waited longingly with faith for many nights. I was sharing this story with a man whose wife had died on hospice. He too had hoped for a visit from beyond the veil. I told him that I had experienced many special spiritual experiences that brought me comfort and I was trying to have faith that my son was alive and well without the visitation I had hoped for. He replied. "Well isn't that what you told him you would do?" "Well yes," I responded as the reality of my own words sunk in. I stopped expecting a visitation.

As a young bishop, Dennis had several opportunities to observe the impact of death on those dying and those left behind. A wonderful sister in our stake lost her husband without warning. He was a prominent and loved priesthood leader and physician. All the outpouring of love, support, and testimony provided much-needed strength to this grieving widow. She was comforted and blessed by others, and her willingness to share her testimony as she entered the mission field kept her grief at bay for a season.

Many months following her husband's death and her honorable release from the mission field, a young adult renting an apartment in her basement called expressing concern. His landlord and admired friend seemed depressed and distraught. When Dennis called this grieving sister and asked if he might be of some assistance, her humble response taught him an important lesson. "Oh, bishop, I would love to visit, but I could never allow others to see me in the waiting room of LDS Family Services." This spiritual sister wanted to be a good example to others who had complimented her on how strong she was. She felt she would disappoint them if she admitted that she was still grieving her husbands' death. She feared that some would judge her delayed grief reaction and need to mourn as a lack of testimony in the Savior's Atonement."

A mother whose daughter was suddenly and violently killed in a high-speed auto-pedestrian accident was confused at first and angry with a God that would take her daughter from her just two weeks before her twenty-second birthday, and only a month before her appointed time to begin serving her full-time mission. With support, prayer, and grief work, this grieving mother eventually achieved spiritual understanding and comfort. She came to believe that God's hands are most often present to sustain and comfort us in our suffering rather than to remove the trials and suffering from our lives.

Well-Meaning Clichés Can Cause Spiritual Injury

After the death of a loved one, family and church members often reach out in a sincere attempt to comfort those left behind. Unfortunately, sometimes their intended words of encouragement cause spiritual injury. Jacob 2:89 warns us not to "enlarge the wounds of those already wounded" with our words.

The following statements and clichés resulted in spiritual

injury according to the grieving members who received them. We might agree with or believe these clichés and some may even be doctrinally true. However, bereaved members frequently list these intended words of comfort as being very hurtful. Some of their specific responses are included in parentheses. These experiences and responses can help us better understand and respect the vulnerability of the newly bereaved.

One family was told shortly after the death of their child that if they did not quit mourning and feeling sad, their child would not be able to progress and do her work in the spirit world.

A mother who lost a child wrote, "The man who drove the car and survived the crash in which my only daughter was killed has several living children. His wife said, 'Look for the silver lining behind your child's death and you'll find it because I have!' She went on to point out, 'You still have your boys.' (Those who have not experienced their own major loss often minimize the impact of such a loss in the lives of the bereaved.)

Another bereaved parent was told by a temple worker, "Your son would be moving out and going on his mission in a few years anyway. This just makes it a little sooner." This mother said, "I felt like I had been slapped in the face."

Those of us who have had a child marry or go on a mission and also lost a child through death know this is a damaging comparison.

Another mother said:

> I was called to be the stake Primary president. The next
> day my daughter away from home at BYU died suddenly. My
> father died eighteen days later. Three days after returning
> from all the traveling and funerals I had my first stake
> leadership training. However, no one in the stake presidency
> said a word to me about how difficult this all must be: having
> a new calling and presenting, so soon after the death of my
> daughter and father. Fortunately I was able to make a good
> presentation. However, the pain from their lack of concern
> has remained with me. Four or five months later, while being
> interviewed by a member of the stake presidency, the subject
> of my daughter's death came up and I got emotional. The
> counselor said, "Oh, you're not over that yet?" I bravely tried
> to explain that it wasn't something I would 'just get over,'
> rather I would learn to cope with it.[1]

A bishop's wife posed this question to a father who had just
lost a child: "Isn't it odd how Heavenly Father takes the most
precious?" This father disagreed as he reflected on the murders,
rapists, thieves, drug and alcohol addicts that die daily.

There are, of course, circumstances when the very young
appear to be called home. The Prophet Joseph Smith taught of
such instances: "The Lord takes many away, even in infancy, that
they may escape the envy of men and the sorrows and evils of this
present world . . ."[2]

It may comfort some to know that their deceased loved ones

are freed from the trials of earth life. However, others may become angry or confused. Some have questioned, "Would God physically take my child or does he allow accidents and disease to occur even among the innocent?"

A well-meaning bishop said, "It's surely a blessing to know your daughter will be spared the trials of this life." Her mother thought to herself, "Send your child. It may seem like a blessing to you, but not to me. I want to raise my daughter here on earth like the rest of you! "

The following additional statements were made by well-meaning members to the bereaved:

"You look like you're doing so well." (She shared later, "You can't see this kind of pain.")

"Well it's not like you don't know where she is!" (Her mother thought, "I would rather be worrying late at night for her to come home by curfew!")

"Well at least he isn't suffering, in a coma, or a vegetable. God loved him enough to take him." His father thought, "Does that mean God doesn't love my aunt who has been in a coma for over a year?" (The "at least" examples usually don't help. They in fact have the tendency of negating another's loss and grief.)

"It was God's will," "God needed him," "His work was done," and, "It was his time."

These statements are all possible explanations for untimely death. Regrettably, even though you may believe one or all of these statements, they usually offer little comfort for those who are grieving.

In a summary, here are some general clichés that might be hurtful to the bereaved:

- We say, "Don't feel bad." (They hear "Don't grieve," which negates their loss.)
- We might say, "It's God's will, he needed them." One mother said, "God has lots of babies, I just had one. I needed her too."
- We might say, "Just give it time" or "Time will heal." (However, time without grief work doesn't usually heal.)
- We might ask, "Did you pray and fast?" (They may hear, "God would have healed me or my loved one if I had prayed more or had enough faith?")
- We might say, "Be strong, put it behind you." (They may hear, "If you show emotion you are weak.")
- We might say, "You just need to get over this." (They may hear, "You're loved one is not worth your sadness and tears.")
- You might say, "She led a full life." (They may wonder, "Does that make me miss her less?")
- You might say, "Just keep busy, the living must go on." (They may feel that you think their loved one is not worth remembering.)

More Helpful things to say would be:

+ I'm sorry you are going through this.
+ I want you to know I care.
+ When you hurt, I hurt.
+ This must be very difficult for you.
+ I can't imagine how you must feel.
+ I'll be there at_____, and bring_____.

The Holy Ghost can, of course, offer comfort through you when you are prompted: "Then can ye speak with the tongue of angels" (2 Nephi 31:13), "Wherefore, they speak the words of Christ" (2 Nephi 32:3). After observing the dilemma of sincere attempts to comfort, a Christian leader warned that inadvertently we often wound those in mourning: "We often bury more people outside the church doors than in the ground when a death occurs!"

In other words, the bereaved are fragile, and at times things are said that hurt them, and in some instances drive them away from our church doors. As previously stated, in most instances, it is safest to simply say you're sorry, and not "enlarge the wounds of those who are already wounded" (Jacob 2:8, 9) with words of intended comfort that minimize the profound grief experienced by those coping with significant loss.

Spiritual Comfort

After the death of a loved one, some individuals receive

spiritual healing from personal impressions, visions, dreams, and visitations. Others are spiritually comforted by their own or another's near-death experiences. These same experiences can also serve as helpful death preparations.

Our disabled son, Cameron, wrote the following poem for a school project six months before his death:

If I Had a Wish

If I had a wish I would wish that I could walk!
I would run and play and all the girls would like me.
See, it's hard to be different in some ways.
Like you can't do your homework without someone helping
     you.
Sports would be fun to do, and I would play basketball.
And I wouldn't miss standing in my prone stander if I could
     walk.
In some ways not walking is good luck because you get to
     drive early! (My Wheelchair) and you don't even have to
     have
     a license.
You also can have a computer all to yourself.
My wish will come true—in the next life!"[3]

The day Cameron died, his special education teacher in Texas remembered the poem he had written earlier about his wishes. We didn't know her well, and she was initially hesitant to share a poem she had written in response to Cameron's poem.

It wasn't until after Cameron's funeral that she decided to share her poetic spiritual impressions. After Cameron's funeral, she quickly went home and returned with her poem. She is not a member of our church; however, she is very spiritual. When she shared the poem, she mentioned that during her fifteen years of teaching, she had never been spiritually touched so profoundly by a student. In turn, reading her poem brought us personal comfort.

She told us that she had trouble sleeping after hearing of Cameron's death. Early that morning she got up and wrote her personal impressions.

The Wish

Written in response to the death of Cameron Ashton and his private wish for his next life.

I felt the breath of death today. It brushed against my cheek, and left me most unconscious, taking thought and words to speak. It left me feeling empty, and lost within myself. It crept about my being like a mouse on pantry shelf. I wandered aimless through the day and half the lonely night, but came a "Great Awakening" at break of morning light. I saw a child in field of green with yellow flowers 'round. He was moving swiftly through the grass on limbs so strong and sound. His laughter rang within my ear as clear as Sunday's bell. His smile did light the broad blue sky and caused the clouds to swell. I watched as one who's privileged eyes had glimpsed through heaven's door, and just as quickly saw it close, revealing nothing more. Then as a wave upon a shore, washes it so clean, my torched mind was cleared to see that this was not a dream. The sorrow felt inside my heart belonged to only me. For how could I be sad for one who's now so free? I swept away a tear that trickled down my cheek, and rose to meet the bright new day that God had given me. I felt witness to a sacred time, not really meant for me. For how often does God grant a wish and allow someone to see?[4]

Cameron talked of death and his next life often. The following is his testimony recorded on videotape six weeks before his death. While Dennis was taping, he had the distinct impression that what Cameron was saying was deeply significant, more than the typical family video session. He worried about Cameron being near death and pled with God in silent prayer that his impressions would not be realized. It took Cameron more than fourteen minutes to meticulously share his life reflections, which after being typed doubled spaced covers less than one page. This is the end of his recorded message. It's the only recorded testimony we have from him.

"I really feel that I can walk in the next life, and that I can talk better. And that I will live forever in the next life after this and that I will see God again. And I get to see my grandma and grandpa again who died a couple of years ago. And you can too someday. I guess I don't have to say anymore. And this is Cameron signing off."[5]

Healing Dreams

Most of us dream about one and one-half hours each night.[6] Dreams often contain elements from our past, present, and sometimes our future. Although we might not remember all that we dream, dreams can bring us significant insight. The scriptures contain accounts of individuals being guided by their, or others,' dreams. One of the most familiar accounts is when Joseph is warned in a dream to flee from King Herod with Mary and baby Jesus (see Matthew 2:13).

One week before Cam's surgery, I dreamed his surgery was over and the doctors said they needed to talk to me. They told me he was having trouble breathing and would have to be on life support and would not be able to live without it. The doctors recommended the removal of life support; however, it was my decision. I went into his room and watched the cardiac monitor move with each thump of his heart. I knew that if I told them to turn off the ventilator, the line on the heart monitor would soon go straight. I thought about my choice for a while. Finally I ran out of the room crying. I could not tell them to unplug my child's life! I wanted him alive! The dream was so real, I woke up sobbing. I felt sad and afraid. I shared my dream with my mother and Dennis. He later related having similar feelings, and several impressions (Death Preparations) that caused him to worry about Cameron too.

At family home evening the night before his surgery, we shared a few of our fears and concerns with Cameron. We didn't want to frighten him so we tried to be reassuring. He had just turned fourteen. Most important, we wanted him to know how much we loved him. I asked him that if something did go wrong and he actually died, would he please try to somehow let us know he was okay and happy in the spirit world? He nodded yes. As I looked at his big tearful brown eyes, I realized this could be a hard promise to keep. I then told him if he couldn't return and tell me (visitation), I would try to just have enough faith to know that he was well. He obediently agreed like he usually did when we made requests of him. Although we had this open discussion during family night, none of us believed it would actually happen.

We'd forgotten about the family discussion and the dream until several days after Cameron's death when my mother reminded us. Remembering the dream brought comfort mixed with guilt. Why didn't we cancel his surgery? Was the dream a warning? However, with time, we chose to believe the dream was a glimpse into our family's eternal future. Over time, the dream became a meaningful death preparation that brought us comfort.

After-death dreams can offer comfort as well. In one dream, I was crying and mourning Cameron's death. I was impressed to get up and read the words to hymn 117, "Come Unto Jesus." The following were the words that brought the most peace and comfort: "Oh know ye not that angels are near you from brightest mansions above?"

VISIONS

It may be difficult at times to tell the difference between a dream and a vision. Visions can occur when we are awake and able to see what is happening; whereas dreams generally occur in our minds while we are sleeping. Visions may occur in the day or at night. The Bible mentions "night visions" (Daniel 2:19).

The vision and revelation received by Joseph F. Smith concerning the redemption of the dead came following the death of his adult son. President Smith agonized for nine months following his son's death. He wondered why he remained alive in his eighties, while his gifted, worthy son in his forties was gone. He felt grief, and through his loss, sought greater understanding. President Smith's grief, prayer, and searching allowed him to receive many comforting doctrinal truths. He died soon after recording his dream that was later accepted as revelation and canonized as section 138 of the Doctrine and Covenants.

The prophet Joseph Smith had a vision where he saw the gates and the beautiful streets of the celestial kingdom. He wrote, "whether in the body or out I cannot tell" (Doctrine and Covenants 137:1). Joseph was surprised to see his brother Alvin in the celestial kingdom. He received the following revelation that clarified how it was possible for his deceased brother to receive celestial glory, even though he had not heard and received the gospel or been baptized. "All who have died without a knowledge of this gospel, who would have received it if they had been permitted to tarry, shall be heirs of the celestial kingdom of God" (Doctrine and Covenants 137:7).

Many enduring adversity wish they could have a comforting vision, but do not. Sister See desired a vision or visit from her deceased thirteen-year-old. When it didn't happen, she turned to the scriptures for comfort. Doctrine and Covenants 24:4 provided comfort and an answer to her plea: "Murmur not because of the things which thou hast not seen, for they are withheld from thee and from the world, which is wisdom in me in a time to come."[7]

Visitations

A visitation is the act of being visited by a deceased person. Although many visitations seem to occur as dreams, some occur while the person is awake and during daylight hours.

One such visitation occurred to a woman seated at her sewing machine. Her mother, who had been dead for sometime, came with an important message for her. She said, "Daughter, you don't know what it has cost me to come to you."[8]

Many have wondered, "What is the cost, and why do some deceased spirits visit while others do not?" Another similar account seemed to be prompted by a deceased individual's strong desire to have her temple ordinances done. She firmly said, "You are the only one I have to depend on. . . . Don't fail in this."[9]

In a therapy session with Dennis, a widower described in detail a visit from his deceased wife. It concerned him much because she had encouraged him to marry a certain woman that they both knew. She explained that he would need someone to help him take care of their children. In the beginning, he wasn't sure he was ready to marry, or that he even wanted to marry this particular woman he hardly knew!

Many who have lost a loved one experience apparitions. Some professionals feel these apparitions are acute grief hallucinations; however, one account seems to rule out intense grief as the cause of a man's deceased wife visiting him eighteen years after her death.[10] His acute grief would no longer be present this long after her death, thus decreasing the possibility of hallucinations resulting from an acute grief reaction.

A comforting experience occurred when a deceased mother who had died from cancer appeared to her grieving daughter and said, "I was allowed to come and tell you not to be worried about me. I don't suffer anymore and I am very happy."[11] This deceased mother made it clear to her daughter that she had received permission to communicate with her.

In one report, 75 percent of parents surveyed who lost children claimed they had an apparition involving their child.[12] On the other side of the veil, some survivors of near-death experiences report asking, while in the spirit world, for permission to communicate with the living and were denied the privilege.

No Visitation

"Blessed are they that have not seen, and yet have believed" (1 John 20:29).

An Amalekite in the Book of Mormon asked why Aaron was allowed to see an angel. "Why do not angels appear unto us? Behold are not this people as good as thy people?" (Alma 21:5). Many members have wondered the same, questioning their worthiness.

Louis E. LaGrand lists possible explanations why some mourners do not have contact experiences with their deceased loved one.[13] He concludes the following: (1) They do not need one. (2) They cannot believe it would occur. (3) Their fear causes repression or suppression of an event. (4) They may have negative states that preclude any positive experience, such as anger, pessimism, or any negative emotion. His 5th suggestion is especially meaningful to us. It is the explanation shared by Paul in the book of Corinthians concerning spiritual gifts. Paul points out that we all have different gifts: teaching, preaching, prophecy, and recognizing angels or spirits. Moroni also lists a number of spiritual gifts, including knowledge, faith, healing, tongues, working miracles, and the beholding of angels and spirits (Moroni 10:9–17). Some of us apparently are not destined to receive the gift of "beholding angels and spirits."

President Wilford Woodruff stated:

> One of the Apostles said to me years ago, "Brother

Woodruff, I have prayed for a long time for the Lord to send the administration of an angel to me. I have had a great desire for this, but I have never had my prayers answered." I said to him that if he were to pray a thousand years to the God of Israel for that gift it would not be granted, unless the Lord had a motive in sending an angel to him. I told him that the Lord never did nor never will send an angel to anybody merely to gratify the desire of the individuals to see an angel. If the Lord sends an angel to anyone, He sends him to perform a work that cannot be performed only by the administration of an angel.[14]

Near-Death Experiences (NDEs)

Many find spiritual comfort from reading the accounts of individuals' near-death experiences. The Apostle Paul describes an out-of-body vision in 2 Corinthians 12:2–4. More than eight million people have reported having NDEs. Some reports of NDEs occur following an illness or accident where individuals lose consciousness, or where their heart has stopped beating, requiring resuscitation efforts. Some individuals experiencing NDEs report finding themselves traveling outside their body. Others report traveling down a tunnel with vibrating sounds. They may view their physical body from above and report the details of their own resuscitation. Many see a light or spirit being. Some are greeted by deceased relatives. Still others describe a brightness and beauty beyond anything earthly. Most profoundly, nearly all report feeling an unconditional, overpowering love and acceptance. The importance of one's love for his fellow man is also reinforced. Many are allowed to visually review portions of their life. Often the life events viewed, which seem to be of greatest importance, are those where they showed kindness and love to other individuals. Personal accomplishments did not seem as significant. It wasn't the honors or praise of men. Rather, it was the love and charity they showed to other human beings. Most NDEs additionally emphasized the importance of obtaining wisdom and knowledge while on the earth.

A few months after our son Cameron died, our forty-year-old friend and neighbor had to have open-heart surgery. I decided to be brave make a strange request. I wished him the best (with such a serious surgery) and acknowledged his fears of a negative outcome. I asked him if he did have complications or had an NDE and found himself in the spirit world, would he try to locate Cameron and give him my love? He agreed without hesitation. After his surgery, he told us that nothing happened and that all had gone well. He was home recovering for a few days when he got very ill and fainted in the shower. His wife took him back to the hospital and the doctors told her that his gall bladder had failed (probably a complication from his previous surgery). He would now need to have an emergency surgery to remove it. While he was on the operating table, they had some problems maintaining his heart rhythm so soon after his open-heart surgery. Gordon soon found himself outside his own body watching the doctors working on his heart below. He was then led to a very large room full of deceased spirits. It didn't take long to recognize Cameron on the other side of the room. He tried to move toward him; however, he was not allowed. He was told he had to go back. He woke up in the intensive care unit. He was weak and ill, but he sent his wife to tell us what he saw. He said that Cameron looked like a missionary and even had what appeared to be a companion with him. He looked content and busy. It brought us great comfort.

Some of the most profound NDEs are reported by children. Young children are innocent, open, unbiased, and they seldom lie about such experiences. Many report seeing and hearing angels or deceased relatives who call them by name, telling them it is not their time to die.[15] Hearing these NDEs has provided many individuals with hope and has increased their faith in what they might experience when they die.

Final Healing: God's Atonement and Resurrection

Hope of a reunion with Cameron has helped Dennis and I endure. However, we still had to walk through a difficult grieving process. At first I questioned as did Job, "If a man die, shall he live again?" (Job 14:14).

I started intense reading, meditating, and praying. I wanted to rediscover how I had gained a testimony of the Resurrection. I studied the book of Job. He also struggled to understand, yet ultimately bore a strong testimony of the Resurrection: "For I know that my Redeemer liveth, and that He shall stand at the latter day upon the earth: And though after my skin worms destroy this body, yet in my flesh shalt I see God: Whom I shall see for myself, and mine eyes shall behold, and not another; though my reins be consumed within me" (Job 19:25–27).

Christ said, "In the world you have tribulation" (John 16:33), but He also said in the same verse, "But be of good cheer; I have overcome the world." He told His disciples, "I go to prepare a place for you" (John 14:2). Our hope and belief in an afterlife does not rid us of our challenges and struggles; however, it can offer us great peace and solace as we endure them. "I am with you always to the end of the age" (Matthew 28:20).

We love the example Christ gave us in the book of John. In fact, we liked the story so much we titled our last grief book after it. Lazarus was very ill. His sisters Martha and Mary had called for Christ to come and heal their suffering brother. By the time the Savior arrived, Lazarus was dead. The shortest verse in the Bible and the title of our book is "Jesus Wept" (John 11:35). Although Christ knew the plan of salvation and also knew he would raise Lazarus, he still had great compassion and "Mourned with those that mourned" (Mosiah 18:9). Those in attendance, witnessing the Savior's tears, said, "Behold how he loved him!" (John 11:36).

In Acts 26:8 we see more proof that God can raise people from the dead. "Why should it be thought a thing incredible with you, that God should raise the dead?"

Joseph Smith said, "If I have no expectation of seeing my family and friends again my heart would burst in a moment and I should go down to my grave. The expectation of seeing my friends in the morning of the first resurrection, cheers my soul and makes me bear up against the evils of life."[16]

"For a trump shall sound both long and loud, . . . and they shall come forth—yea, even the dead which died in me, to receive a crown of righteousness, and to be clothed upon, even as I am, to be with me, that we may be one" (Doctrine and Covenants 29:13).

The first Easter after Cameron's death, I had to give a lesson to the Young Women organization on the Resurrection. I knew it would be difficult because my grief was still so fresh. I reviewed the lesson the night before and went to bed. I had a special dream that continues to bring comfort to me now, many Easters later:

There was a large-colored rock similar to something you'd see in St. George, Utah. From behind it came Cameron walking briskly toward me . . . no wheelchair which he had spent his fourteen years in . . . he had a smile on his face (usual for him). I was walking toward him quickly, knowing that it was the Resurrection and that I was greeting him after many years of separation. I was eager to get my arms around him; however, before I reached him I awoke to the name of a hymn. The hymn was "Come unto Jesus." I jumped from my bed to find the hymnal and read the words of the hymn:

"Come unto Jesus, Ye heavy laden, careworn and fainting . . .

he'll safely guide you unto that haven where all who trust him may rest . . . Come unto Jesus, he'll surely hear you if you in meekness plead for his love." And as previously stated, "Oh, know ye not that angels are near you from the brightest mansions above?"

Yes, I knew! I knew Cameron still existed even though I hurt and missed him. I knew he was near and that I had claim on the Resurrection, and that if I followed Christ's example and lived worthy I would see him again.

I received even more comfort from reading Revelation 21:4, which says, "And God shall wipe away all the tears from their eyes; and there shall be no more death, neither sorrow, nor crying, neither shall there be any more pain; for the former things are passed away."

Attending the temple in behalf of Cameron brought one additional spiritual comfort from his loving Father in Heaven. Dennis had hoped, like many others coping with the loss of a loved one, for a miracle sign, visitation, or at least a reassuring dream. The Prophet Elijah had a similar desire as he sought a dramatic miracle from God to change hearts and prevent the physical and spiritual deaths of those in his stewardship. Instead, he learned firsthand from the Lord that the most convincing witness to the righteous is often much more subtle. "And the Lord passed by, and a great strong wind rent the mountains, and brake in pieces the rocks before the Lord; but the Lord was not in the wind: and after that wind an earthquake; But the Lord was not in the earthquake:

And after the earthquake a fire; but the Lord was not in the fire: and after the fire a still small voice" (1 Kings 19:11–12).

This still small voice came at a sacred moment in the temple. As I mentioned before, we had hoped, like many others coping with the loss of a loved one, for a miracle sign, visitation, or vision of some kind. Rather, it was a miracle moment of complete reassurance concerning the immortality of the human soul. That witness came at a sacred location at the completion of Cameron's temple endowment.

Once again we consider the words from the movie *Man's Search for Happiness*: "Life's greatest test comes with the death of a loved one, and without faith in the immortality of the soul, the separation of death looms forever comfortless."[17]

Fortunately, God has not left us comfortless. He has promised: "I am the resurrection and the life and he that believe in me though he were dead yet shall he live" (John 11:25).

Notes

1. Ashton, *Jesus Wept*, 183–4.
2. Joseph Smith, *Teachings of the Prophet Joseph Smith* (Salt Lake City: Deseret Book, 1976), 196.
3. Ashton, *Loss and Grief Recovery*, 141–2.
4. Ibid., 145–6.
5. Ashton, *Jesus Wept*, 167.
6. E. Linn, *Premonitions, Visitations and Dreams . . . of the Bereaved* (Incline Village, Nevada: Publishers Mark, 1991), 72.
7. Joselli K. See, "I Prayed to See My Son," *Ensign*, January 1977, 62.

8. J. Heinerman, Joseph Lyon and Assoc., *Spirit World Manifestations* (Salt Lake City: DBA Magazine Printing and Publishing, 1978), 84.

9. Ibid., 86.

10. M. R. Sorenson and D. R. Willmore, *The Journey Beyond Life*, Vol. 1 (Midvale, Utah: Sounds of Zion, Inc., 1988), 65.

11. Ibid., 44.

12. Oprah Winfrey Show produced by Harpo Productions, Inc., Chicago, October 8, 1993.

13. Louis E. LaGrand, *After Death Communications: Final Farewells* (St. Paul, Minnesota: Llewellyn Publication, 1997), 185–86.

14. Leaun G. Otten and C. Max Caldwell, *Sacred Truths of the Doctrine & Covenants*, Vol. 1 (Salt Lake City: Deseret Book, 1982), 63.

15. M. Morse, *Closer to the Light* (New York: Villard Books, 1990), 159–61.

16. Smith, *Teachings of the Prophet Joseph Smith*, 296.

17. *Man's Search for Happiness*, 1964.

CHAPTER FIVE

Murder, Suicide, Disaster, War, and Terrorism

THE DEATH OF A LOVED ONE USUALLY REQUIRES adjustments and grief work. When someone loses a loved one to murder, suicide, terrorism, war, or a natural disaster, the adaptation may be more complicated and the duration of adjustment lengthened.

Murder

Murder is a serious sin. It can compromise the victim's agency and shortens their life experience and probation time. Those who lose a loved one to murder not only have to deal with the loss of their loved one, but additionally the traumatic way he died and a judicial system that may seem more concerned with the perpetrator's rights than the victim's. It can impair and assault our sense of safety, justice, and trust. Combined, these factors often complicate and prolong the grieving process, making it more difficult for some to function again at home, work, church, or even in society.

A grieving mother approached us after we spoke at a bereavement conference stating: "A few years after the death of my husband, my daughter was murdered. I am the one who found her battered body in her apartment. Words cannot describe the intense trauma, pain, loss, and anger that I feel. I felt I had pretty much recovered from my husband's death when my daughter died. However, I can't seem to recover from this one. It's been five years now and I am still in therapy."[1]

Death caused at the hand of a murderer becomes complicated because it could have been prevented. People feel intensely violated when someone purposely takes the life of their loved one.

A mother whose daughter was raped and murdered shared the following: "It's been seven years . . . you never forget it, you just learn to live with the pain. It's something you just don't get over."[2]

For healing interventions see *But If Not, Volume I.* Professional therapy is available through LDSFS and other licensed professional counselors.

Suicide

Those who take their own lives are usually in tremendous mental, emotional, or physical pain. We must remember God is their judge. We may not understand the depth of pain and hopelessness associated with suicidal thoughts and acts. Those left behind often struggle with difficult questions, confusion, and guilt. They often ask, "Could I have done something that would have made a difference?" Their mourning process can also become complicated and prolonged.

Bruce R. McConkie taught, "Persons subject to great stresses may lose control of themselves and become mentally clouded to the point that they are no longer accountable for their acts. Such are not to be condemned for taking their own lives. It should also be remembered that judgment is the Lord's; and he in his infinite wisdom will make all things right in due course."[3]

Each year in the United States there are over thirty thousand suicides reported to the Centers for Disease Control and Prevention. Imagine the intense pain numerous family members and friends experience as they mourn those who chose to end their lives. Included amid those reported deaths were four children under nine years of age. More than five hundred thousand adolescents and the same number of adults attempt suicide annually. It is sad to think that five to six thousand teens take their own lives and five times that number of adults die annually. It is discouraging and alarming that suicide is the fifth leading cause of death among five- to fourteen-year-olds.[4]

Most teen suicides stem from drugs and alcohol. Out of every four high school students, one will use marijuana. Most adolescents get their first drug without cost. The biggest teen killer in the United States is alcohol.

One woman expressed her fear that alcohol and drugs played a role in her son's depression:

> My son stays out late. He is always missing his curfew. He is seventeen and we have tried everything to encourage him to keep his curfew without much luck. I don't sleep well worrying about him. He has also shared with us that he has been involved with smoking and had some experience with alcohol. He does not seem to have a testimony or spiritual feelings. He is not interested in church, going only because we pressure him. We have talked with him, taken away money, the use of the car, etc., without much improvement. I fear he is suicidal.

Depression can lead to suicide when depressive symptoms go unrecognized, especially in children and teens. Others won't admit they have a problem and refuse medication, often for fear of looking weak.

Dennis's mother committed suicide on her fiftieth birthday. She left a distraught husband and two young sons still at home. Her life history contributed to her depression and suicide. Her mother moved out of the home at an early age, requiring her to quit school before completing the eighth grade to help raise her younger siblings and care for their home. Her father died at a young age after an extended illness. Over time, she began to experience phobias and suffered from severe panic attacks. The combined abuse of alcohol and prescription drugs brought about other serious health problems. Her addictions, mental illness, and deteriorating health eventually intensified her feelings of frustration and hopelessness.

Dennis wrote, "After my mother committed suicide, the hardest part for me was watching the pain my father experienced, and knowing my younger brothers would be raised without a mother."

M. Russell Ballard said, "The act of taking one's life is truly a tragedy because this single act leaves so many victims: first the one who dies, then the dozens of others—family and friends—who are left behind, some to face years of deep pain and confusion."[5]

A woman whose nephew committed suicide said, "My nephew very much wanted to serve a mission. He tried on two occasions to stay at the MTC. His depression overcame him and he returned home discouraged both times. Soon after he committed suicide. We were all devastated. His father continues to suffer with addictions and debilitating symptoms from his grief."

A mother in a bereavement group was struggling as she tried to cope with the death of both her children. Her oldest son had died of cancer. On the first anniversary of his death, her daughter, who was still grieving his death, committed suicide. Following such a devastating loss, she said, "The pain and sadness is just too much for me to handle. I really would like to join my children in the Spirit World. I think about it a lot."

Other bereaved parents of children who committed suicide

have stated to us years after their losses that they were surprised to still be alive yet proud to have made it through!

Guilt is a common emotion for those siblings left behind. Notice the guilt this young adult felt after her brother committed suicide.

"My brother's last words to me were 'Help me.' Three weeks later, he committed suicide. I was left haunted. Haunted by my failure as a sister to save my only sibling's life. Haunted too by a wide range of emotions, which I chose to bury for twenty-seven years. I have been frozen in the grief process."[6]

It's important to know that once someone has made up his mind to take his life, no amount of talking, interventions, or effort on our part alone will guarantee that they will not attempt suicide. Consequently every threat and suicidal gesture must be considered valid and potentially lethal.

For healing interventions see *But If Not, Volume I.* Professional therapy is available through LDSFS and other licensed professional counselors.

Natural Disasters

When a natural disaster occurs we often hear the question, "Did God cause this?" This thought process can cause hurt, anger, and spiritual injury for those who may feel they are being punished by God.

There is some scriptural and doctrinal evidence that the Lord on occasion has controlled the weather. President Spencer W. Kimball said, "The Lord uses the weather sometimes to discipline his people for the violation of his laws."[7]

God said to the children of Israel,

> If ye walk in my statues, and keep my commandments, and do them; Then I will give you rain in due season, and the land shall yield her increase, and the trees of the field shall yield their fruit. And your threshing shall reach into the vintage, and the vintage shall reach unto the sowing time; and ye shall eat your bread to the full, and dwell in your land safely. And I will give you peace in the land, and ye shall lie down, and none shall make you afraid: . . . neither shall the sword go through your land. (Leviticus 26:3–6)

Most natural disasters are equally devastating to both the righteous and the unrighteous, the saint and the sinner. The rain truly does fall on the saint and sinner, "For he maketh his sun to rise on the evil and on the good, and sendeth rain on the just and on the unjust" (Matthew 5:45; see also 3 Nephi 12:45).

The Prophet Joseph Smith taught that "all flesh is subject to suffer and the righteous shall hardly escape; . . . it is an unhallowed principle to say that such and such have transgressed because they have been preyed upon by disease or death."[8] The Apostle Paul was aware of this reality when he spoke of the Savior. He said, "Though he were a Son, yet learned he obedience by the things which he suffered; And being made perfect, he became the author of eternal salvation unto all them that obey him" (Hebrews 5:8–9). No one would suggest that the Savior's sufferings were the result of transgression on His part.

There is also scriptural evidence that the weather on occasion can be tempered as people repent: "When heaven is shut up, and there is no rain, because they have sinned against thee; if they pray . . . and confess . . . and turn from their sin . . . then hear thou in heaven, and forgive the sin . . . and give rain" (1 Kings 8:35–36).

Losing a loved one to murder, suicide, terrorism, or a natural disaster brings unique and often complicated issues for grieving individuals to consider.

When Dennis traveled to Indonesia to train mental health workers on loss and grief, he found many there who believed that God was punishing them through the tsunami. This thinking caused significant pain and suffering to many who had lost loved ones. Some had lost everything; not only their loved ones, but homes, land, and personal possessions. Such trauma to their mind, body, and spirit would not heal easily. LDS Humanitarian Services provided millions of dollars worth of assistance that included everything from body bags, washing machines, housing, and motorcycles, to training professionals on providing loss and grief counseling. Fifteen professionals consisting of physicians, psychologists, and clergy received training from Chris Anderson and Dennis, both LDS Family Services staff sent by Church Humanitarian Services.

Once trained, these professionals would provide the loss and grief training to counselors who in turn would go out and provide therapy to grieving individuals and families. One physician receiving this mental health training asked Dennis why a small Christian church ten thousand miles away could care and provide resources to a people of another faith. He assured her that the Church members he represented worship the same God, mourned over their burdens, and desired to provide comfort in the midst of their adversity. She asked if she might visit Utah some day to learn more about LDS Humanitarian Services and meet staff from the University of Utah and Brigham Young University.

War and Terrorism

We are blessed to live in America where we enjoy freedom. It comes at a great cost. We are grateful for those who leave their loved ones and safety to protect us. Our hearts go out to those families who are grieving for a loved one lost to war or terrorism. When a death was preventable it can increase the intensity and duration of grief symptoms.

A few years ago Dean Bird and Dennis had the opportunity to help coordinate LDS Humanitarian and Family Services relief efforts to Kosovo refugees seeking asylum in Albania. While comforting the refugees, Dennis and Dean witnessed and experienced firsthand many sad and tragic challenges. After speaking at a missionary conference where they shared ideas on helping families deal with loss and grief, two missionaries offered to introduce Dennis and Dean to a family they had recently made contact with. The family escaped across the border of Kosovo into Albania after experiencing catastrophic losses. The next afternoon Dean and Dennis met with the family and heard their horrific story. Soldiers had accosted the family as they participated in a large family gathering. All the men were taken outside of the house. Women and children were ordered to draw the blinds, remain inside, and not make any attempt to look out or leave the house. Within a few minutes, which seemed to last for hours, gunshots rang out into the dark, cold evening. The oldest member of the family, who told the story, had just lost her husband, son, and grandson. The living members of the family remained in either their house or the basement of a neighbor's house for nearly a month, leaving only briefly in the evenings to secure a scant ration of food and water.

Dean and Dennis found it difficult to listen but knew as professional therapists that the first step to recovery is allowing the process of mourning as the bereaved share their personal, unique pain. The feelings that come through expressing one's deepest hurt and loss are often healing. They were both surprised a day later when the missionaries returned to invite Dennis and Dean back to visit the family. The Kosovo family indicated that they trusted and felt safe with these humanitarian workers sent by the LDS Church. They asked if they could share additional details surrounding the death of their loved ones.

In the second meeting, the family revealed that they had smuggled a videotape out of their country that chronicled their horrific experiences. The preservation of the tape was important enough to overcome their fear of being caught with such evidence as they escaped in the dark of night across the border to freedom and friends.

The video included scenes of mothers, wives, and daughters as they kissed and patted the heads of all the deceased men and boys who had been ruthlessly taken from their family circle on that awful night. The bodies had been gathered to the home in the darkness, where they had been washed, clothed, and eventually secretly buried. It was important that their loved ones' mortal bodies not be burned or mass buried by the soldiers. A tattered yet sacred piece of hastily torn paper indicated the precise location of each loved one's makeshift grave.

Dennis and Dean found exposure to such carnage difficult, yet realized that allowing the family to share in detail their personal burdens provided a small measure of comfort and meaning to the grieving family.

Alma's preaching at the Waters of Mormon remind us of the sacred promises we make as members of Christ's Church to be willing to bear one another's burdens, provide comfort, and perhaps most important, mourn with those who are mourning (see Mosiah 18).

It is amazing how resilient the human soul is. Most can and do survive catastrophic and horrific events.

Many of the refugee shelters and tents that Dennis and Dean visited were filled with young children who had lost their parents. One hot afternoon as they were standing in a tent city of over one thousand refugees, Dennis and the other humanitarian workers witnessed an act of kindness, which helped them realize what they could do in return to help lighten the refugees' burdens.

A senior humanitarian missionary, exhausted by the heat and many hours on his feet, found relief leaning against a steel pole. An elderly Kosovo refugee sitting on a large cinder block brick noticed the missionary's exhaustion. He stood up and walking backward, dragged his makeshift chair to the humanitarian missionary. His cinder block brick represented the only seat in this community of over two hundred tents. The humanitarian workers were touched by this act of compassion and quickly identified what they could do to help, in a seemingly small way, to bear another's burdens.

A few days later the humanitarian workers returned to this tent city with a gift. They had purchased hundreds of plastic chairs. When the children saw the missionaries approaching, they surrounded them, pulling on their clothing.

The translator told them that the children were expressing thanks for the generous gift and pointing in the direction of their families' tents. Each child feared that there might not be enough of the chairs for each family in the camp. Returning weeks later, the missionaries learned that the school tents were the first to receive chairs. They were additionally impressed as they walked down the many rows of tents. Each family had received one chair and that chair was prominently placed in each clean, makeshift home. The valued gift was equally shared among all the families. No one in the camp had claimed more then one chair for his family. The teachers' and mothers' burdens were lightened a little that day as they were now able to rotate from their chairs to the ground while they taught and cared for the young children.

The humanitarian missionaries also had the opportunity to visit families from Kosovo who were housed by Albanian families. Arbin, a convert to the Church and interpreter, invited LDS Family Services staff to his home to meet a refugee family staying in his home. Several months earlier, Arbin's father had a surprise visit from a Kosovo business associate that he traded with one day every other year. His business associate stood at Arbin's door and said, "I've lost my home in Kosovo." Arbin's father responded without hesitation, "My home is your home." His associate then confessed that he had not come alone; other survivors were secluded outside the apartment. These twelve extended family members did not want to embarrass their potential host. After all, his home consisted of only three small bedrooms, a living area, and kitchen. It was barely enough room for the home's four current occupants.

When the representatives of Family Services arrived, they were invited into Arbin's former bedroom. Arbin had given his room to five of the thirteen houseguests. For the past three months he had been living a week or so at a time with different members of the Tirana Branch so there would be room for these afflicted guests.

With eighteen refugees plus family members and visitors in the small bedroom, there was only room if everyone sat shoulder to shoulder against the walls. Dean Bird and Dennis contemplated what they might say to express their deep concern. They felt inspired to let the host family and refugees know how much they loved them and were deeply sadden by their suffering. Dennis also felt impressed to mention that there were thousands of members of our Church worldwide who would have gladly come in their place if they were given the opportunity. The senior member of the Kosovo family responded apologetically, "But do you know we are not members of your church?" Dennis and Dean's response, without hesitation, was, "Yes, we know. But we believe we all worship the same God." Their honest response brought peace and instant friendship.

Our charge as members of the Church to love all of God's children was reflected in the words of the Prophet Joseph Smith more than 150 years earlier: "A man filled with the love of God would not be content with blessing his family alone, but ranges through the whole World, anxious to bless the whole human race."[9]

He also said regarding the duties of members of the Church toward all their fellow men: "He is to feed the hungry, to clothe the naked, to provide for the widow, to dry up the tear of the orphan, to comfort the afflicted, whether in this church or in any other, or in no church at all, wherever he finds them.[10]

Following Dennis and Dean's expressions of love, concern, and common brotherhood, the family spontaneously and in unison expressed three times aloud their appreciation by bowing their heads and repeating, "Thank you very much, thank you very much, thank you very much." From that moment on, there were no barriers of race, color, religion, or custom that could separate those present from the love of God. Before they left that evening, Dennis and Dean, now referred to as honored guests, were invited to have refreshments from the families. They both declined initially, recognizing how very little food the two families had to eat. Ultimately they realized that the refugees' grief work included giving and sharing as well as expressing thanks for what they had not lost, including their own lives.

That evening every one ate from one small plate, gratefully passed like a sacrament tray from person to person. The plate held one apple cut into very small slices. Next, the special guests were offered a small, carbonated orange drink. Dennis soon realized that only five individuals had a glass. He quickly finished his drink and returned the glass to the serving tray. The glass was quickly removed from the room by one of the teens, where it was washed, refilled, and shared with the next oldest member of the gathering. Dennis has expressed how the reverence and spiritual healing of that moment will never be forgotten. A few days following Dennis and Dean's visit, two of the teenagers present that night began missionary lessons with the full-time elders in that same small, humble home.

The death of a loved one usually requires adjustments and grief work. When someone loses a loved one to murder, suicide, terrorism, or a natural disaster, the adaptation may be more difficult and the duration of adjustment period lengthened. However, the Lord has assured us that he will be with us: "I will not leave you comfortless" (John 14:18); "Fear not, let your hearts be comforted . . . waiting patiently on the Lord" (Doctrine and Covenants 98:1–2). For coping and healing interventions see *But If Not, Volume I.*

Notes

1. Ashton, *Jesus Wept*, 21–22.
2. ———, *Loss and Grief Recovery*, 169.
3. Bruce R. McConkie, *Mormon Doctrine*, 2nd ed. (Salt Lake City: Bookcraft, 1966), 711.
4. G. Anderson, *Our Children Forever* (New York: Berkley Books, 1994), 186.
5. M. Russell Ballard, *Some Things We Know, and Some We do Not* (Salt Lake City: Deseret Book, 1993), 8–9.
6. J. Stanford, *The Forum Newsletter,* Association for Death Education and Counseling, March/April 1999, 15.
7. Kimball, in Conference Report, April 1977, 4–5; *Ensign*, May 1977, 4.
8. Smith, *Teachings of the Prophet Joseph Smith*, 162.
9. Joseph Smith, *History of The Church of Jesus Christ of Latter-day Saints*, Vol. 4, ed. B. H. Roberts (Salt Lake City: The Church of Jesus Christ of Latter-day Saints, 1976), 227.
10. *Times and Seasons*, March 15, 1942, 732.

Conclusion

DISABILITIES, ILLNESS, OR THE DEATH OF A LOVED one can bring profound feelings of loss and grief. Grief is hard work. It is the work of thoughts and feelings. In the beginning phase of loss we may not have much control over our thoughts or feelings. However, as we acknowledge and actually pursue our "grief work," using the tools we discuss in Volume I, we can gain increased control and peace. By doing our grief work we are choosing to become survivors rather than victims of our circumstance.

Like many of you, Dennis and I have lived a life full of both joy and adversity. We cared for our disabled son, Cameron, for fourteen years before his sudden and unexpected death. We experienced infertility, miscarriage, and the death of a full-term infant. We raised another son who struggled with Attention Deficit Disorder and later became trapped in his addictions. We have learned how quickly life can leave us as we have buried all four of our parents. One parent died of suicide at fifty and another of heart disease at age sixty-one. Our oldest son, when he was only in his thirties, had a colon mass removed which resulted in severe complications and several major surgeries over a two-year period.

Our hope is that *But If Not Volume I, Volume II,* and *Volume III* on loss and grief can give you ideas for coping with the "but if nots" that will inevitably come your way, those times in your life when God's hands are there to sustain you rather than take away your adversities. We have determined in spite of our personal trials that "our God whom we serve is *able* to deliver us. . . . *But if not,* be it known . . . that we will not serve thy gods, nor worship the golden image" (Daniel 3:17–18; emphasis added).

Rather than becoming bitter when we face life's but if not's, we hope to become better as we endure. We are grateful for the gift of the Comforter, spiritual gifts, and tender mercies that help individuals endure extreme trauma in their lives. We have discovered that the human soul is resilient and most individuals will accommodate and adjust to loss across time. "But they that wait upon the Lord shall renew their strength; they shall mount up with wings as eagles; they shall run, and not be weary; and they shall walk, and not faint" (Isaiah 40:31).

May God bless you on your life's journey.

About the Authors

Joyce Ashton is a registered nurse and certified bereavement advisor. She is currently the Director of Spiritual Care for Rocky Mountain Hospice.

Dennis is a licensed clinical social worker, former bishop, and assistant commissioner for LDS Family Services. He is currently the agency director for the LDS Family Services Centerville and Layton Utah agencies. Dennis was a guest on KRNS and KSL following the Salt Lake City Trolley Square shooting and Crandall Canyon Mine disaster. He has also appeared on *Living Essentials*.

Joyce and Dennis teach at BYU Education Week and are frequently broadcast over KBYU-TV. They have authored the following books: The *But If Not* series, *Jesus Wept, Loss and Grief Recovery*, and also have several published online and journal articles and book chapters.

Joyce and Dennis are the parents of six children, four of whom are living, and have several grandchildren.

0   26575 52408   6